The Birds Eye Book of Home Freezing

Christmas and Boxing Day fare assembled from pre-prepared ingredients stored in the freezer

THE BIRDS EYE
BOOK OF
HOME FREEZING

Chiquita Sandilands

With drawings by ROY DEWAR

CASSELL · LONDON

CASSELL & COMPANY LTD
35 Red Lion Square, London, WC1
Melbourne, Sydney, Toronto
Johannesburg, Auckland

First published 1971

I.S.B.N. 0 304 93664 2

Printed in Great Britain by
Cox & Wyman Ltd.,
London, Fakenham and Reading
F. 1270

Contents

For Francis, Jane-Elizabeth
and Keir, who helped me.

Illustrations

A Birds Eye View

The idea of freezing food has been with us in Britain for almost a quarter of a century. Nearly 2% of all we eat today is quick-frozen by commercial manufacturers and two-thirds of all householders own a refrigerator.

But the idea of freezing in the home is still very new. In 1965, fewer than 30,000 homes could boast one of these gleaming white giants. Five years later they were taking up floor space in every electricity showroom and another 300,000 had been purchased. Few electrical appliances have caught the popular imagination quite so dramatically.

Birds Eye have for many years argued the case for the simplicity and naturalness of quick freezing and were delighted when Cassell invited them to sponsor this new book on the art of home freezing. There are skills that have to be learned just as, fifty years ago, there were skills to be learned in the art of bottling and home preserving.

Chiquita Sandilands has written a book that is at once entertaining and informative. Quick freezing is a highly complex science, but she has been careful not to confuse the 'do it yourself' home freezer with technical detail that only a food technologist would understand. We have been happy to lend our resources and experience to Chiquita Sandilands and we hope this book will make a contribution to the better understanding of what is still the most efficient and natural method of food preservation.

Special thanks are due to the following for their help and co-operation in producing this book: Miss Margaret Leach, M.B.E., Head of Home Food Preservation Section, University of Bristol Agricultural and Horticultural Research Station; Miss Jenny Salmon, Company Nutritionist, Birds Eye Foods, Ltd.

NOTE

Where an asterisk appears in the first seven chapters, this denotes that the recipe for that item appears in the section Freezer Facts, Figures and Recipes.

1 Declaration of Intent

Of all the revolutions that have taken place in the post-war years, only one has done nothing but good to those involved in it. This solitary example of the advantage of action over discussion is the home-freezer revolution.

Without demonstrations, bomb throwings, throne topplings or barricades, some of the worst domestic tyrannies have been quietly put down for ever.

The balance of power in the home has been delicately readjusted to the everlasting benefit of the revolutionaries. The job of catering for a family, of two people or five or ten, is no longer directed by such unalterables as early closing days, dock strikes, labour disputes, seasonal shortages, foreign pestilences, and the impossibility of stretching the day beyond its quite inadequate span of twenty-four hours.

The home-freezer revolution has achieved what none of the others has managed—freedom in an area where the word has scarcely applied before. Freedom from the shopping rush, the cooking rush, the what-the-devil-can-we-have-for-lunch rush, the rush to shop while the children are in school, the rush to cook at the end of a working day.

The only pity of it is that so few of the potential revolutionaries have seen fit to join in. This book is an unashamed— no, more than that—a deliberate and determined recruiting campaign for the forces of revolution. At the last count, it was shown that about two homes in every hundred in Southern England, and half that in the North, possessed a home freezer. Now why should this be?

It may be because the mechanization of the home has been a long, slow process, blotted in many places by the shortcomings of many prototype household appliances.

Most of the docile robots now in service have thoroughly

1

shameful antecedents, with a history of explosions, fusings, floods and fires. Positively the only one that has never had any peculiarities, that came into the world properly house-trained, is the home freezer.

So the reasons given by anti-revolutionaries for their non-participation are usually circumstantial—but no more valid for all that. The reasons come in stock forms.

Some say: 'We haven't got room'. Anybody who checks their space against the available range of home freezers will very likely find they *have* got room.

Some say: 'Freezers are too expensive'. They are not—a freezer adequate for a family costs about one third as much again as a comparably-sized refrigerator, and more quickly justifies its outlay.

Some say: 'We don't use much frozen food'. You don't have to be wild about fish fingers to have use for a freezer. Home freezing largely means cooking the food you like, when you like, and eating it when you're ready.

Some say: 'The family eats out so much during the week that I only cook properly at week-ends'. This is a reason in itself for having a freezer. How pointless it is to spend the two family days slaving over a hot stove, when everything except the salads can be prepared between Monday morning and Friday night.

A small but significant group of diehards, and those mostly men, will not consider a home freezer because 'freezing makes food tasteless'. This, if you will bear with a moment of dogmatism, is absolutely, completely and utterly *wrong*.

It can only be a relic from the earliest freezing times, when nobody quite understood what they were dealing with. Restaurants, particularly, froze food wrongly and served it wrongly—over- or under-cooked and *tasteless*. The food got the blame instead of the restaurateur, who deserved it. An oven can much more readily make food tasteless by over-cooking it than a freezer will by freezing it, but nobody uses that as a reason for sticking to hay-box cookery. Freezing does not *make* food anything but extremely cold during its storage period.

The most frequently offered reason, though, is 'I've never thought of having a freezer'. There is but one answer to that—'It's high time you did!'

Why a freezer?

A freezer is not a luxury, or a status symbol, or an extravagance. It's a practical necessity in a family home, and a piece of domestic and economic sense. It fits into and completes the pattern of contemporary living more than any other consumer

2

durable—that expression always makes me think of a vast lady in welded corsets grimly pounding at a timid man from the gas works, though I realize that a durable consumer is quite a different thing.

Where the freezer makes sense is in the extra dimension it brings to the non-stop job of feeding a family, whether there are two members or twelve. This work was probably easier, in a grim sort of way, forty or fifty years ago. Then, the house-keeper knew exactly who would be at home for breakfast, lunch, tea and supper, and at exactly what time.

The family, for their part, knew exactly what they would be given to eat according to the season of the year and the time of the day.

All the mother had to do—all?—was stick by her cooking range and turn out frightening quantities of that dreaded commodity 'Good, wholesome food'.

It is significant, and an argument for freezers, that the good wholesome food of yesterday is the stodge of today— the porridge, the heavy puddings, the interminable stews, the duff, the enormous cooked breakfasts, the obligatory, stupefying Sunday lunch, and the huge knife-and-fork teas.

Many of us don't eat that way any more, so there is no particularly good reason for continuing to operate as if we did.

The pattern of eating that has evolved in the post-war years makes redundant the martyred mother-figure, glower-ing and muttering into her seven steaming cauldrons while her hoggish dependants sit banging their spoons.

It could certainly be shown that the *per capita* consump-tion of food has radically changed since the days when the squire stuffed himself to apoplexy while the peasantry practically fell down dead from starvation at his gates.

Variety – the spice of life

But what has thankfully been lost in sheer dyspeptic quantity has been triply compensated for by variety. And the prime use of a home freezer is to bring variety right under the hand of the one who is preparing the meals. You don't know until you've tried it how different that is from having to make the choice from the supermarket display a day or a week earlier, or worse, forgetting to make it at all.

The choice, too, is immediate. Speed is another factor in our changed pattern of living. We eat more quickly and less regularly now, because there are more available interests and activities to be packed in than ever before.

She who possesses a home freezer, and operates it with a pennyworth of forethought, which is all it needs, is never

3

again in the awful position of answering: 'You'll just have to wait!' to the urgent shriek from husband or child: 'I've got to be at the club/Cubs/choir practice/the station/Timbuktu in ten minutes, and I'm *starving*!'

Neither does she have to stand tapping her foot and turning down the heat under drying gravy when half the family has already eaten and the rest are either caught in a traffic jam or kept in detention at school again. If you have no idea who will be home when, you feed the first lot and rely on the freezer to provide for the latecomers. If you happen to be the latecomer yourself, it doesn't matter.

Meals at your finger-tips

A freezer puts an end to the grisly business of rushing home from work or an outing, dropping your hat into the vegetable basket as you grab the potatoes, dratting with impatience at the meat that won't cook, slapping hungry hands away from the loaf and wishing you'd stayed at home and been a slave so that everybody should feel guilty about you.

Until we all have microwave ovens, which won't be this side of the year 2000, I imagine, nothing will replace the home freezer in helping to keep the impossible pace we have for some reason set ourselves.

The Birds Eye Book of Home Freezing, then, is a one-end-to-the-other exposition of the what and why and when and how of freezing food at home. It is for the guidance of people who own freezers and the persuasion of those who think they might, or should, or very soon will.

There is as much advantage in home freezing for women who have jobs outside the home as there is for the others whose work is inside it—and the same goes for the book, as well.

Call it a revolutionary's handbook, if you like, but remember that the most interesting place to be during a revolution is up ahead where the action is. And as you will see, home freezers are more meaningfully revolutionary than Castro will ever know how to be.

2 First Catch Your Freezer

Just about the only household on earth where it could truthfully be said that a home freezer would be merely something else to dust is that of an Eskimo family camped permanently above the snow-line within sight of the North Pole.

Even then, it would be a thoughtful Eskimo husband who provided a freezer within the igloo, thus saving his snub-nosed little wife from having to put on her furs and go outside to get the pudding off the roof. The electricity supply might be a problem, but pehaps they could work out something with a windwheel. They're said to be a resourceful race.

In every other household where the outlay can be contemplated for cash or for credit, a freezer should quite reasonably be given priority over most other household culinary appliances. Assuming that you already have the front-line basics of cooker, sink, refrigerator and storage space at the kitchen end of the house, a freezer is the logical back-up.

It is the only ancillary object whose function cannot be undertaken by other means. You can wash the clothes in the launderette until you can afford a washing machine, and do the dishes in the sink until a dishwasher descends by way of a legacy or saving sixpences in a whisky bottle. You can, if you have to, thump away at the butter and sugar with a wooden spoon instead of using a mixer.

But you cannot preserve fresh food for more than a week or two in a pantry, in a domestic refrigerator, or anywhere else except in a home freezer. Neither can you keep a permanent, ample supply of commercially frozen food, or indulge in the pleasure of buying when the food is cheap and plentiful and eating when it's dear and hard to come by, or save time, energy, fuel and thought by cooking for a week or a month rather than for the next meal.

5

These are the main practical reasons for owning a home freezer, and buying it before anything else that the uninitiated persist in calling 'luxuries'.

A freezer is a second pair of hands, or even a third and fourth at crisis periods like Christmas, birthday parties, or being laid out by the flu. It represents freedom from the tyranny of clock and stove, malevolent inanimates, always at odds with each other and for ever using you as a frantic go-between. With a choice of any one out of a dozen meals waiting politely in a freezer, you have the better of them.

Ownership of a freezer adds a hedonistic dimension to life that you wouldn't otherwise know was there. You can buy twelve pounds of strawberries when they're red and luscious, eat as many as you want with your fingers all sugary, yet know that the rest will come out of the freezer one dark night in November and you can have the same high-summer ecstasy all over again.

A freezer is as much help to a wildly disorganized housekeeper as it is to those rather formidable ones who not only make lists but actually remember where they put them. Even perfectionists can sometimes stumble and they, no less than the disorganized, can cover their errors and omissions by keeping Mr Birds Eye's products always to hand. Saints and sinners alike no longer need an alibi.

Having so unequivocally established that the home freezer is the one thing that must not wait for the ship to come home, one is left to decide what kind of freezer to choose, where to put it, and estimate what it will cost to buy and run.

What a freezer will (and will not) do

You must be clear about what you are buying. You are not buying a refrigerator, which is an appliance for keeping food in cool conditions. Neither are you buying deep-freezing equipment. Deep-freezing is a process employed commercially, involving the use of air blasts at ultra-low temperatures of −73°C. (−100°F.).

If you choose an appliance designated anything but a home or food freezer, exactly that, it may not be primarily intended for the freezing of fresh food from room temperature downwards.

The frozen food storage compartment of a household refrigerator is designed only for storage of foods already commercially quick frozen—the star marking system on packaging indicates the maximum recommended storage time. The temperature in the compartment is maintained at anything from about−18°C. (0°F.) up to −6°C. (21°F.).

The same applies to a combination or refrigerator/freezer

6

◀ Breadcrumbs and herbs make an ideal stuffing for Beef Olives. Serve with a brown sauce from the freezer

1
Thaw frozen chicken completely before cooking. Serve with rice and curry sauce from the freezer

2
Smooth pâté should be covered with a layer of butter before thawing and serving

3
Commercially frozen foods and raw meat assembled for packing, labelling and freezing. Make sure that joints are cut to a usable size before freezing

4
This pasta dish 'Lasagne al Forno' is made with tomato sauce, cooked minced beef, white sauce, grated cheese and herbs, all from the freezer

1

2

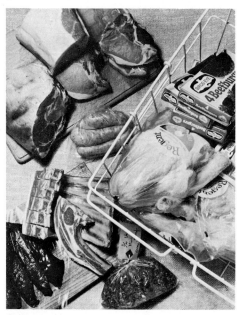

3

4

This has two doors to avoid temperature rise in the low-temperature section which is normally capable of freezing food.

A conservator is a frozen food compartment on a large scale, and belongs where it is mostly seen—in shops or ice-cream parlours. It operates between −18°C. and −20°C. (0 to −4°F.). It is adequate for storing ice-cream or commercially quick-frozen foods, but not normally designed to freeze food by its own efforts.

By definition, a home freezer is an appliance designed to reach a temperature lower than −18°C. (0°F.) and to freeze a specified quantity of food from room temperature within twenty-four hours. It is also capable of storing commercially frozen foods.

Fast freezing

Some of the large-size freezers on the market have a 'fast freeze' compartment. Fresh food is put into a walled-off section in one part of the freezer, and a switch operates the fast-freeze mechanism.

In fact, the switch by-passes the thermostat which regulates the working of the freezer motor, allowing it to run continuously during freezing time instead of intermittently as it does for storage. The partition provides an enclosed space which becomes cold enough to freeze food rapidly so that natural flavour and texture are retained. Almost the same effect can be achieved in any freezer by turning the thermostat control to its coldest setting.

Choosing the right size — mini, midi, maxi

The price you will pay for a home freezer depends on its size, measured in cubic feet.

A single person *could* manage comfortably with the smallest practicable size—one and a half to two cubic feet. Families big and small, ardent cooks, gardeners or farmers can go by stages right up to sixteen cubic feet and never regret it.

As with a refrigerator, it pays to buy a freezer at least one size bigger than you think you'll ever need, and two sizes bigger if your family is still growing and you can fit in both a freezer *and* the children.

If you have a large garden, estimate the quantity of fruit and vegetables you give away or put to compost because you can't eat, bottle or jam them in time, and use that as a basis for size.

Consider your entertaining programme—regular, enthusiastic or reluctant—and be swayed by that, too. If you don't enjoy cooking you can get by with a smaller freezer than you would need if you did. If you do enjoy it, get an *enormous* one.

The largest freezers make the best economic sense.

But their size is something to be reckoned with, and not everybody has that kind of space. A sixteen cubic foot freezer, fully loaded, can weigh up to a quarter of a ton. It would be prudent to have the load-bearing capacity of the floor beneath it checked by a builder, and probably not risk it on anything but a foundation floor.

A four cubic foot capacity freezer may cater for the short-term needs of a family of two or three on the basis of half the space for long storage of out-of-season or specially prepared food, and the rest for day-to-day needs.

But once you become hooked on freezing—and you will, you will—the constant juggling of packages and pots will begin to drive you mad.

The day will come when the lid or door won't close and you are left standing with an armful of homeless dishes clutched to your rapidly chilling bosom, and you will be obliged to invest in a second model of the same size or change the freezer for a larger one.

Freezers for small kitchens

You may have to buy two freezers instead of one in any case, if you have two small spaces that won't combine to make one large area. I have one four cubic foot freezer in the kitchen and another in our noisome cellar, but it makes the capital outlay one-third as much again as an original purchase of a freezer in the six, eight, ten or twelve cubic foot range.

The freezer doesn't necessarily have to be in the kitchen. Some modern kitchens are more like pigeon-holes—friends of mine have just sued their builder because it was discovered, too late to do much about it, that their sup. mod. kit. could have a sink or a door, but not both. The prospective lady of the house quite reasonably refused to make the choice between being bricked up inside for life, or washing the dishes on the patio—so there may not be room in some kitchens planned or constructed in very recent times.

With some juggling of movable fittings, though, you may be able to fit a freezer in a place where you didn't think anything would ever go. At this point, you may have the decision made for you about whether you have a chest-type freezer, with a top-opening lid, or an upright type with a door opening outwards like a cupboard, or even a small model to stand on an existing surface or fridge.

The long and the short of it

A four to four and a half cubic foot chest-type may go into an otherwise inaccessible corner. It needs only the space of its own base—about two feet square. But small people may have difficulty in reaching to the bottom of the freezer—it

8

would never do to be found upside down among the frozen vegetables, with icicles in the eyebrows and feet waving wildly, so it would be wise to try a few practice dips into the showroom model.

If you have more headroom than floor space, an upright freezer or combination (refrigerator/freezer) may be the obvious choice. The loading space is then contained in height rather than depth or breadth, and the contents are marginally easier to get at, but you do have to have room for yet another opening door.

The long, large freezers of the chest-type are usually fitted as standard with several wire baskets that drop into place along the top edge of the chest below the lid. These hold several layers of packaged food, easily lifted out to reveal the lower echelons without scavenging about and jumbling the entire contents. Smaller freezers can take one or two baskets according to the size of the chest, but these are usually bought as extras.

If you use the freezer several times a day, as you eventually will, I think a basket is essential. If you are a long-term storer for high days only, you can do without it. If you run one freezer for daily use and a second for long-term storage, then the second freezer can do without a basket. You save a little bit of space and a little bit of money, which always helps.

Where to house your freezer

In trying to fit a freezer into an uncooperative kitchen, you need not be ridden by the ancient maxim of not having a refrigerator near a source of heat—cooker, washing machine or boiler—but it *is* more economical if you can keep it away from all sources of heat.

Modern insulation effectively keeps the heat where it is intended to be. All you have to provide is a clear two inches of space between the condenser and the nearest adjoining surface—including the wall at the back of the freezer. This modest amount of space is necessary to allow air to circulate around the condenser so that heat extracted from the food can be dispersed.

The freezer would work even more diligently than usual if you rammed it hard up against the cooker and pressed the boiler against its other side. The motor would work longer than normal and the electricity bill would be slightly higher than it need be. Anyway, two inches isn't much to spare such a willing servant.

If, after all the measuring and scheming, you still can't fit a freezer into the kitchen, it doesn't matter so terribly much. Like one of those sad old aunts who used to do all the dreary

9

mending in return for bed and board, a freezer will make do with the humblest accommodation.

It might be fitted in the bit of wasted space under the stairs, or in the dining-room if the décor isn't so formal that it would stick out like a sore thumb. It might go in a covered back porch all among the wellingtons and walking-sticks, in the dark bit of lobby so often found between showy art nouveau front and gloomy stucco back in older houses. I have known freezers put in spare bedrooms, but this would seem to have problems beyond the one of having an extra cause to climb the stairs.

You could always put a chintz cover and a dainty ornament on it when people come to stay, but the guests might well wonder why you kept darting up to their chamber, and take to carrying their valuables about with them. Even worse, they might wonder what guilty secret you were keeping in the wardrobe.

Probably the most accessible and suitable place for a freezer, outside the kitchen, is an integral garage or one of those enviable laundry rooms. The garage will not be a good idea if you have to go outdoors to reach it—that *would* restrict the menu when it was raining stair-rods.

If a freezer has to be outside the house, or in the basement, it should still never be exposed to damp. Apart from being detrimental to the finish of the casing, damp conditions over a long period may reduce the life of electrical and mechanical components.

Warning devices

If the freezer is housed in a garage or porch it should have a warning device of bell and/or buzzer fitted to operate some-where obtrusive *inside* the house. If you are within earshot of the thermostat's reassuring click, you will soon notice if a power cut or a careless hand on the electricity switch has turned off the current.

A wide piece of sticking-plaster fixed right across the switch and marked in big letters 'Do Not Touch' should prevent accidental switching off. With none of these pre-cautions, the first intimation of disaster you have might be the sight of a three-foot deep puddle when next you open the freezer.

Some freezers are fitted with a lock. The bigger the freezer, the more important it becomes that it should be *kept* locked, unless the household is composed entirely of trustworthy adults—trustworthy in the sense that they won't become peckish and help themselves to something you were nursing for future use.

A big, unlocked freezer is a definite danger to small children. If they can get as far as lifting the lid, they can go further and topple in.

Apart from these once-for-all safeguards, a freezer is the most undemanding of all household aids, and among the cheapest to run. Running costs for individual homes depend on the local electricity charges, but each cubic foot of freezer will use just about three to five units of electricity a week. An eight cubic foot freezer is therefore likely to cost about 25p (5s.) per week to run.

Defrosting

Defrosting a freezer is usually a twice-yearly job, but it can be cut to once a year if you are careful never to leave the door or lid open for longer than the time it takes to retrieve the package you want. It could equally well be a four to five times a year job. Every opening introduces warm air making extra frost form round the inner walls.

Uprights sometimes need more regular defrosting than chests, but an excessive build-up of frost around the door indicates a poor seal, and this should be investigated without delay.

The obvious defrosting time is when supplies are low and the remaining food packages can either be farmed out to a home-freezing friend nearby, or put into the coldest part of the refrigerator for a few hours.

Then you switch off the current—pulling out the plug as well, in case some obliging busybody switches it on again—lift up the lid or leave the door open, and put a plastic bucket full of hot water on the freezer floor. The loosened frost is scraped away with a plastic or wooden spatula. Never on any account use a metal scraper, or you may wreak awful havoc by cracking or even splitting the inner casing and damaging the network of pipes within.

When the inside is clear of frost, wash the inner walls with a solution of one tablespoonful of bicarbonate of soda to four pints of water, and dry thoroughly—you won't want a thin layer of ice to form as soon as you switch on again.

Turn on the current when the job is done and close the freezer for a couple of hours to lower the temperature. Then put the food back.

You can take it with you

A freezer packed with food will stand moving from one house to another if the journey is not going to take more than a few hours between the old electricity point and the new. The close-packed contents will remain more firmly frozen than if the freezer were only partly-filled.

Even a power cut, unless of the most dire kind involving

11

broken cables and much digging in the road by the Electricity Board, will not necessarily affect already frozen food inside a *closed* freezer.

Power cuts

If the worst happens and the whole district is plunged into darkness, *do not* keep on opening the freezer to see if everything is going into involuntary liquidation.

If the cut looks like persisting for more than a few hours, help the freezer's insulation by covering it closely in several layers of blanket. The bigger the freezer, and the more it contains, the better its chances of survival even up to or beyond a full twenty-four hours.

Freezer insurance

If nothing happens after that time, you do stand to lose the lot—which, apart from fire, burglars or flood, is a reason in itself for insuring the freezer's contents. Some insurance firms offer a freezer policy at about £2 per annum for every £75 worth of food, some cost much more than others, and some won't take the business at any price. This, like so much else, is a matter of shopping around for the best bargain. Just don't forget to do it until after the power cut.

It is most unlikely that anything will go radically wrong with the refrigeration system of a new home freezer. One cannot say as much for a second-hand or even reconditioned model, in spite of any or all guarantees.

A cut-price freezer, unless bought in a regular sale from an irreproachable dealer, should be approached with caution—nay, with downright suspicion. You can never know just where a second-hand or bargain-price freezer has been, or what was done to it while it was there.

Mechanical troubles

The motor/compressor is normally a sealed unit, which means that there is effectively nothing to go wrong in normal use unless the thing has been wrongly assembled or tampered with. If this happens to a new freezer you will soon find out and be able to fall like a ton of bricks upon the manufacturer. A shark dealer in second-hand models, supposing he is there when you go back to confront him, will merely show his six rows of teeth and ask you what you expected for that kind of money?

All things being equal, a freezer bought from a dealer of repute and a manufacturer of experience will simply trundle along until it dies of old age—and freezers are yet too recent a development for anybody to know just how old they can be if they try.

I just hope mine won't be called to Higher Service before me, that's all.

3 Using Your Freezer

The first home freezer I ever knew personally belonged to Mrs. Renwick, a splendid North Country woman married to a Sussex farmer. It was a majestic appliance, a full twelve cubic feet, occupying a room all to itself at one side of the low-ceilinged, many-cornered, shadowed farm kitchen that I shall continue to covet till the day I die.

The freezer, at the time of our meeting, was stocked on supermarket lines—very prudently, since Love's Farm is over a mile from the nearest road, and Farmer Renwick has been known to ski right over the hedge tops on his way to fetch the post and papers in January. It was a very poem of orderliness, that freezer, all the contents neatly wrapped, labelled and stacked to be identifiable at first glance.

It seemed to me that I should never be a satisfactory freezer owner if *that* was how things had to be done. I could not but reflect on the annual shambles of my Christmas parcel wrapping, my utter inability to keep both ends of a package closed and fasten string round the middle at the same time. Labelling is not my strong point either, as one of my aunts will testify.

She once travelled ten miles by bus to take the golf stockings she received one year and exchange them with an uncle who had spent a miserable holiday explaining away the merry red panties that had arrived for him. The gift cards had somehow become muddled, and his wife thought he had been mixing with the wrong people entirely.

With such a background, I couldn't see myself making a very good job of wrapping up a codfish. And the possibilities of disaster inherent in confusing labels on sweet and savoury, flesh and fowl, were together almost enough to put me off the whole idea.

So I give thanks publicly now to Mrs. Renwick, whose words should by rights be printed on slips of paper and put into new freezers along with the book of instructions and the guarantee. She said: 'It's a bit of a taskmaster sometimes, a freezer, but you just have to go steadily along and you soon get used to it.'

How true! Pretty well everybody, at the outset of a home-freezing career, views the empty cavity in just about the same light as a new-born baby. In the same way that one tends to think the baby is going to stop breathing any moment, so one wonders timorously whether the freezer is going to stop freezing the minute one's back is turned.

Exactly as one can't leave the baby to its own devices for half an hour without turning it over or up or giving it something to drink, there is this great urge to lift the lid, prod the packages to see if they have frozen or are just sitting there mocking one.

A freezer is not a refrigerator

In the beginning, too, there is a touch of uncertainty about whether a home freezer is only a very determined refrigerator. Be clear about this. It isn't, and you don't have to wait to find out by putting the remains of Sunday's chicken into the freezer instead of on a dish in the fridge. You will have a fright when it has frozen solid and you have to open a can of spaghetti for Monday's lunch.

A domestic refrigerator is for today, tonight and tomorrow, for milk, butter, cream, eggs, lettuce, salad dressing, minor leftovers, bacon, cooking fat and cheese.

A home freezer is for next week, next month and next season, for nearly every known perishable, cooked or raw, except hard-boiled eggs, bananas, very fat meat, mayonnaise, and shellfish, unless it was lively enough to come into the house originally under its own power.

Food can be eaten directly from a refrigerator. Foods other than ice-cream from a freezer have to be thawed by direct heat in the oven, or by leaving in the comparative warmth of the refrigerator.

You can shove foods into the refrigerator and leave them there with no firmer covering than a saucer or a piece of foil. You *can* do the same with food in a home freezer, but the results will be lamentable in almost every case.

The worst that can happen in a refrigerator is having the butter tainted by foreign odours from a neighbouring cheese or fruit. Mishandled food from the freezer, though, will be in a much more depressing state—dry, shrivelled, colourless, and so confused about its identity that nobody will be able to state with certainty whether they are eating asparagus or cow heel. But you would have to be an awful idiot to let this happen. It hasn't happened to me yet, which amply proves the point.

So continue to treat the refrigerator like the first child, the one you learned on, and view the home freezer as the sibling who gets the benefit of your experience and doesn't cause half the anxiety.

The whole idea of having a home freezer is to release you from the nitty-gritty work of the kitchen—the daily peeling and preparing and slicing and wondering whether you can serve cold lamb *again* without endangering the stability of the home. From the very beginning you must treat it as an adjunct to your previous, familiar routine, not as a demanding, foot-tapping monster waiting to make a monkey of you.

At the same time, you must make allowances for its special qualities. The food you consign to a freezer will be expensive —*all* food is expensive—and some of it may be there for any length of time up to a year. Throughout the storage time, it will be subjected to very low temperatures indeed. Various changes will come about in its composition during the freezing and thawing processes. Your first consideration is to be sure that the changes are kept to a minimum and given no chance to affect the food to the point where it changes perceptibly in flavour or structure.

Prepare with care

For this reason, above all, you must be careful—but not obsessively so, unless you just happen to be that kind of person—about preparing food for the freezer.

The food must be thoroughly and carefully packed. Most manufacturers recommend that only one-tenth of the freezer's total capacity should be used to freeze fresh food in any 24-hour period. That is, no more than two pounds of food per cubic foot of freezer space.

If the freezer is overloaded with fresh food, the packages will take an undesirably long time to freeze right through.

The quicker the temperature of food is lowered, particularly through the zone 0° to $-5°$ C. (32°–23°F.), the less chance there is of physical damage to food tissues. In other words, food frozen rapidly tastes and looks better than slow frozen food.

Never, ever, put a warm dish or box or package in the freezer. Not only will it soften anything it touches inside, but it will temporarily raise the cabinet temperature too far for the good of food already frozen, and so take a longer than desirable time to freeze through.

Pack fresh food in the fast-freeze compartment or close to

the walls of the freezer, where the temperature is lowest. Keep the packages apart from each other to allow the circulation of cold air between them. When they are completely frozen, they can be stacked or packed closely.

The purpose of careful packaging is fivefold—to stop the food from drying out and suffering 'freezer burn', resulting in nasty whitish marks on the surface; to exclude as much air from around the food as possible, because the presence of air promotes the development of oxidation products which make the food taste and look unpleasant; to protect delicate food from being squashed; to stop flavours from mingling inside the freezer, and to use all the space to best advantage.

Packaging

High density polythene, heavy-duty kitchen foil, non-stick and greaseproof paper, square or rectangular containers of plastic or waxed cardboard, freezer tape and plastic-coated wire ties for bags are the freezer-owner's armoury.

You can order a large and costly consignment of 'special' freezer bags made of thick, moisture-vapour proof polythene, waxed cartons of many shapes, freezer tape and labels specially treated to withstand extreme cold, and little tubes of ties in several colours.

All these, except the tape and labels and possibly the waxed cartons, can be washed and re-used many times over. If not lined with polythene bags the waxed cartons are inclined to go soggy or tear, or both, during thawing.

Containers on the cheap

When you are more experienced in freezer ownership you may make numerous economies in packaging materials. Yoghurt, cottage cheese, cream and margarine containers made of plastic are very useful for sauces, purées and soups, etc. If they do not have re-usable plastic tops, aluminium foil can be used and sealed with freezer tape. It helps if your dairyman sells cream in plastic pots with lids, not the waxed ones with cardboard tops that break your fingernails before they sink silently into the cream. Well washed and dried, these can hold their own quite easily against any purpose-made container for smallish quantities of purée, single portions of sauce, and home-made baby food.

I show my gratitude to the margarine manufacturer who puts his product in lidded containers, by buying the same brand all the time and considering it a bonus to be able to freeze so much so often in the package. Margarine containers stack into each other most obligingly in the freezer. By pushing smartly upwards with the thumbs at the bottom, the contents can be shot out in one piece.

Hang on to one-pound sugar cartons, too. With their aid,

16

you can achieve the desirable rectangular pack that saves freezer space like nothing else. Press a polythene bag smoothly down into the corners, fill and freeze the whole thing, then lift out of the carton to reveal a frozen brick.

Cartons for soups and sauces

One of the most adaptable freezer containers I have ever found is the waxed milk carton which holds about a pint of sauce or soup, allowing for headspace when the frozen food expands, and something like twelve ounces of fruit or meat. It is said that cartons can be bought with the milk in, washed and used for the freezer. I don't believe it, but this may be because my eldest child always opens milk cartons with one blow from his penknife. It's all I can do to get the milk as far as the jug, never mind salvaging the container.

If you have a similar problem, you can still buy a gross of cartons from a well-disposed wholesale dairy for about sixteen shillings. They sound like a storage problem, but are not. They stack so closely that a gross will fit into one large carrier bag hung from a convenient hook in a cupboard— I keep mine like that, anyway.

If only I could find the insouciance to ask people for their empty individual jam-pots in tea-rooms, and not feel I have to explain myself, I should have a better collection of containers for frozen herbs. Never leave such things behind when you have tea on a train or in Fuller's—indeed, deliberately *have* tea in order to obtain them. Nothing so useful is produced for freezer owners exclusively.

Sealing tape

I have found rolls of masking tape from the paint merchant more effective than many other sealing materials. This is meant to be stuck on windows to keep drips off the glass when the frame is being painted. Not only does it hold fast to frozen packages, but it has the added advantage of being brown-paper coloured and plainly seen—none of that groping round with thumbnail to find the join.

If you buy heavy-duty polythene sheets or bags you can be sure they are moisture-vapour proof whereas some cheaper ones may not be. If they are thin they are likely to be punctured easily.

Polythene bags

It will pay to look about you for a shop specializing in plastics of all kinds—drainpipes, ceiling tiles and what-not. These often sell polythene bags in quantities of a hundred or more, showing a vast saving over more modest purchases.

The only snag here is the possibility of buying too many bags all the same size. Ideally, one should keep a small store of small bags, a large store of medium, and a small store of large. Nothing is more tiresome than being obliged to enfold four spare fish-fingers in an acre of polythene. You invariably open the packet at the wrong corner and let them fall on the floor. And if the cat is quicker on the grab than you are . . .

Labelling

Special freezer labels may sometimes fall off and get lost just as readily as ordinary jam-pot labels. I am not convinced that every single thing in a freezer should be labelled by name, though the date of freezing is useful to know in case of long-term storage or items with a limited freezer life.

A bean is a bean and, in a transparent polythene bag, is recognizable as such by colour and shape, and if you can't tell which is a chicken and which a piece of topside, you have troubles that the rest of us cannot conceive of. Opaque containers should, of course, be labelled, so should different substances that look alike in the frozen state, and any made-up dish that is wrapped in opaque material or could be confused with another. Frightful to find yourself eating curry when your taste-buds were geared to steak and kidney.

Writing the identification with a chinagraph pencil on waxed or plastic containers is more reliable than any label. Transparent containers and food overwrapped in polythene bags are secure if the identification is written with the marker on the sticky side of the label and fixed to the *inside* of the bag. Just remember to put the marked side upwards during freezing.

One economy isn't worth making—cheap or give-away plastic boxes are very seldom usable in the freezer. Unless you have found a bargain in discontinued plastics from the best firms, the lids will not fit tightly enough to provide a seal without the additional security of tape. You are better served by the faithful polythene bag.

How this battery of objects is to be used is largely dictated by common sense, but I would be the last person to suggest that this admirable quality is the only one necessary.

Packaging hazards

One of the most common-sense people I know, in the first freezer flush, bought fourteen pounds of best pork sausages from a butcher whose reputation had travelled the several miles between her house and his shop. She wrapped them most carefully, placed them in the freezer, and announced: 'Now we can have some of that man's lovely bangers whenever we fancy them.'

The sausages were duly fancied one cold night when the family had all been to the cinema—but alas! My unhappy friend found that there is absolutely no gentle way of separating one pork sausage from another, let alone one pound from fourteen, once they have enjoyed a few days in a home freezer. The whole lot had fused together until they looked and felt like one of those old-fashioned steel radiators. They separated them eventually by brute force, using the coal hammer wrapped in a tea towel.

Most people have at least one horror story of this kind—my own concerns a dozen lamb chops. But at least one ever after remembers to separate items destined to be cooked or served individually.

Chops, sausages, steaks, fish, sliced or jointed poultry—all these must be rigidly segregated from their fellows. This can be done by putting one piece or one portion in the bottom of a polythene bag, folding the bag upwards from the bottom over the second portion like a Swiss roll, and so on to the top, finally enclosing all in a large bag. You can equally well put a double piece of greaseproof paper, polythene or cellophane between successive portions, but this involves neat work with scissors and the folded bag does just as well.

It won't matter very much if you put two trout or two cod steaks cheek by jowl, or a couple of chops, since it is likely that they will constitute one meal or one portion. A pound of sausages won't hurt if the string is put longways into a bag and the bag folded back on itself to divide the quantity and speed up the eventual thawing. But take more liberties than this with items that are going to freeze solid, and you too may have to resort to the coal hammer.

A similar hazard exists in putting soft packages, or bags with any damp on the outside, against the wall of the freezer—or worse, against the wires of a freezer basket. They stick. The longer you leave them, the tighter they cling, until you are reduced to prising them loose with a steak hammer. This is bad for the look of the food, bad for the freezer, bad for your temper because your hands freeze and you don't realize you have also bashed your fingers until they begin to hurt several minutes later.

Make a habit of wiping all packages dry with a piece of kitchen paper before freezing them.

The rest of the packaging rules justify themselves in practice. Whatever you are packing for the freezer, make it as airtight as possible. Press the wrapping *closely* round fish, meat, poultry, using the flat of your hand to push air pockets out of the top of the bag and hold it closed while you fasten the neck with a wire tie.

Any sharp edges—chop bones, chicken joints, and shanks —should be wrapped with scraps of polythene, greaseproof paper or cellophane before packing, or they may break not only their own bonds but probably those of their freezer neighbours as well. Foil is not good for this kind of wrapping. It can turn itself into an extra cutting edge if subjected to pressure from other items inside the freezer.

Packing fruit

Soft fruit, which would hardly benefit from being pressed with anything, can be put into loosely-tied bags and frozen for an hour or so spread flat on a wire cake-cooling tray. By then, each berry will be just firm enough to withstand the air being pressed out by a gentle patting movement from open fingers, and then the bag tightly fastened. This results in flat, floppy bags of fruit which can be protected from crushing by placing them in rigid polythene boxes. Once frozen the fruit *can* be shaken down to form a compact package if you prefer.

Packing bread and cakes

Bread, sandwiches and everyday cakes will not resent being bagged willy-nilly. Neither will pastry, though if it goes straight to the freezer from the pastry board and escapes from a loose wrapping, it may cleave to something more delicate and be a nuisance in the end. A very frail layer cake, intended for a birthday some time hence, should be given the full treatment—a foil pie-dish or fibre plate for support beneath, the whole thing placed in an air-tight plastic box or tin.

Packing vegetables

Whole or sliced vegetables, except broccoli or cauliflower sprigs, can be packed loosely in a large polythene bag for freezing and then packed more compactly. The vegetables will then be free-flowing. The two exceptions need tender handling and should be packed from the start in rigid polythene or waxed boxes with interleaving between layers.

Packing liquids and semi-solids

Liquid or semi-solid food, soup and stock, fruit or tomato purée, should ideally be packed in waxed cartons or plastic containers. But to save space—or if you simply run out of containers at the wrong moment—they can be bagged, the bags lining a rectangular sugar or dried fruit carton to produce a regular-shaped frozen brick. The trick here is to bag them smoothly. If you freeze a squashed-up bag of anything slightly runny, it ends up in accordion pleats and there is no way of telling where the bag ends and the food begins. You must then rip and pull the polythene away, but little bits will escape you. As sure as eggs are eggs, the person who gets an overlooked piece of the packaging locked between their teeth at table will be the one who doesn't approve of freezers *anyway*!

If you use cartons, leave between a half and one inch headspace between the top of the food and the top of the carton to accommodate expansion of the food during freezing. Likewise with the bag—fasten the neck about an inch clear of the food, enough to let it expand without locking round the tie.

Packing pre-cooked food

Pre-cooked food can be ready for thawing, heating and serving if frozen in an ovenproof cooking dish after cooling. But this is a prodigal use of freezer space, to say nothing of taking a casserole or pie dish out of circulation for an indefinite period.

It pays to master the fiddling art of lining dishes with foil and putting the cooked food in this inner container for freezing. The theory is that you should be able to lift the foil-wrapped food cleanly from the dish and keep it in the freezer overwrapped in a polythene bag.

How dangerous is theory at times—I once had four assorted and awkwardly-shaped pots lounging in the freezer. Two were narrower at the top than the bottom so the solid foil package wouldn't come out at all. The others were locked in a frozen embrace because some gravy had escaped between dish and lining.

The clever thing to do is to leave a *wide* margin of foil all round the outside of the dish, cover the surface of the food with a separate piece of foil and put the lid on top, having used your fingernail and a piece of kitchen paper to wipe every single trace of goo from the two adjacent surfaces.

When you take out the frozen foil package, you simply fold the overlapping foil right across the top, and the food is sealed within. The reverse applies to thawing—put the whole lot back in the dish, heat it and take the foil out when the food has begun to thaw or at the end of the cooking time.

One warning I would give. It is difficult to work this trick with a tart or pie. You can't, unless you have extreme dexterity or three hands to fold and pleat the foil to fit the pie plate most exactly and hold it down *without any gaps underneath* while you line in the pastry and filling. The pastry gets into the inevitable gaps and won't come out without maiming the pie and forcing you to pretend you always serve them that funny shape. Better to admit defeat and always use foil plates—though why nobody will ever make a foil plate the same size as a normal one, I do not understand.

Things like that become important when you begin to use a home freezer. You come to see why frozen food firms never go in for fancy packaging, but stick to squares and rectangles. With their resources, they can achieve what home freezers can only aim at—symmetrical packages that stand one upon the other to use up every last inch of cold space.

This ideal is nearly impossible to achieve outside a commercial world, but when you have been using a freezer for a while you will find yourself becoming very miserly over space.

You may be able to get eighteen pounds of evenly-packed frozen food into one cubic foot of freezer space. Lumpy, uneven packing can cut this total by a quarter, meaning that you are paying good money for cooling all that air in the holes between one lump and the next.

This is the ultimate reason for careful packaging and neat stacking in a freezer—sheer economy, allied to ease of handling. Never, I pray, let yourself get to the stage of wondering if there is another bag of strawberries down there *somewhere*, or did you finish it off when the Joneses came to dine?

Never let yourself be found grovelling about among heaps of this and that, spreading the contents of half a freezer over the kitchen table—you'll forget to put something back, for sure. I once lost a prize crab that way—looking for something not lost but probably gone before.

Keeping a Proper List
If ever there was a case to be made for keeping a Proper List, the home freezer makes that case. Don't make a list on a shopping pad, because you will lose it. Don't make a list on a scrap of paper and keep it in the drawer, because you will throw it out. Don't make a list and pin it on the wall, because it will become yellow and curled and finally blow away.

Buy one or more pieces of plastic laminate, with a hole for hanging up by a bit of string, and fasten the end of the string to some immovable object near the freezer. Buy a chinagraph pencil and string that on as well.

The object of this exercise is to make your list too unwieldy to vanish, your pencil not convenient for somebody to borrow when they want to leave a note for the milkman or write down a phone number. To stop children from drawing funny men on the list, dangle it down between the wall and the freezer, not on the open side.

Write the quantity of each item contained in the freezer—strawberries, 12 lb.; mince, 4 lb.; pastry, 6 lb.; bread, 3 loaves; and so on. Every time you use one package or dish or loaf, rub out the last total and write in the new one. When the whole lot has gone, erase all figures but leave the name of the food to act as a reminder when re-ordering or cooking for the freezer.

The story of my redcurrants will serve to illustrate the need for a list. It was in December that I thought of using those currants, but currants there were not.

I turned out *two* freezers in the search, peered into bags,

◀ A delicious ratatouille prepared from a selection of fresh and frozen vegetables

1
An assortment of frozen vegetables available through the Birds Eye Home Freezer Service

2
Frozen roast and piped potatoes shown here with commercially frozen potato products

3
Mushrooms being prepared for freezing by blanching in hot oil

4
Pancakes taken from the freezer, layered with cooked spinach and covered with a cheese sauce and grated cheese provide an interesting supper savoury

1

2

3

4

accused the entire household of gluttony compounded by dishonesty, and came near to the point of claiming on the insurance for burglary.

I had quite forgotten, you see, that the currants had been turned into jam the previous July.

4 Freeze it Yourself—Some Do's and Don'ts

In the first few years of its history, home freezing has had to live down more old wives' tales than any other human activity, with the possible exception of childbirth.

All kinds of hazy race-memories survive from our fly-ridden, pre-refrigeration past. Everybody over the age of forty will be happy to tell you the story of their cousin who died of oysters, of their best friend who was never the same after eating pork in July, of the man who knew a man whose dog fell down and never rose again after its second mouthful of stolen rabbit.

Freezer myths and legends

There are people to be met even now, with the consumption of commercially frozen food alone having more than quadrupled in the last fifteen years, who view even the pastorally innocent frozen pea with grave suspicion. They 'just don't trust it'. It isn't *fresh*. You don't know where it's *been*.

You can try to impress such disbelievers by giving freezing the respectability of passing time—tell them it is now nearly a hundred years since the first cargo of refrigerated meat crossed the Equator and didn't kill anybody when it got here. They only say 'Huh!'

If one were to be swayed by conservative tradition, the question of what to freeze and what not to would never become a matter of debate. Water alone would be acceptable, as long as it had been boiled for ten minutes.

If you can rid your mind of all ancient preconceptions, or if you are lucky enough not to have any, you will get far and away more value from your home freezer than if you were hung-up on antiquated saws about months with an R in them.

Look at it this way—if mankind had never discovered that

24

food can be preserved for future consumption, by smoking, drying, salting or heating or with preservative substances, the human race would hardly have got up off its knuckles. The various Ice Ages, famines, floods, cataclysms, crop failures and migrations would have eradicated *homo* before he had a fair chance of becoming properly *sapiens*.

Some myths exploded   Home freezing is to the 1970s what salting was to our far forefathers—the most refined method of preserving fresh food known to the era. Packaged dried foods are not comparable in our own time, since that kind of preservation is never likely to become household practice.

Freezing, moreover, is basically the most natural and desirable form of preservation. Nothing is taken out of food to stop it from decaying. Nothing whatever is *done* to cooked or raw food, beyond reducing it to, and keeping it at, a temperature of −18°C. (0°F.). This has the effect of retarding the chemical changes which spoil food when it is left exposed to air at normal temperatures.

Freezing is about the easiest way of preserving almost *anything*, in one appliance and using one set of utensils and materials.

Nobody who has once put up a few jars of plums, made a pound or two of bramble jelly or salted a bean, is ever again quite free of the primitive urge to preserve food against the hard winter ahead. Never mind that the hardest winter catches most of us only between the front door and the car, that Birds Eye stockists and bulging supermarkets stand at every corner—it makes no difference.

Year after year, you get this atavistic prod towards protecting your brood from starvation after the harvest. It is an urge that costs the inept very dear in terms of fruit scorched and stuck to the jam pan, therms and units of heat rolling away in pursuit of the elusive 'jelling point', pickles turning black because you don't *have* a silver knife to peel the onions, the breadboard buckled beyond redemption after being put in the oven to hold the sterilizing jars, tea towels bursting into flames in the same cause, fingers wrinkled and scorched from hot glass and metal, even damaged feet when the hazardous 'test for seal' proves negative and the jar drops from its lid like a free-falling parachutist from his hatch. However, do not let this gruesome catalogue of disaster depress you. The accident-prone, like the poor, are always with us, and the survival rate in kitchens encouragingly high!

When one thinks of the lost freezing years, one could

weep. I *do* weep when I remember falling down the stairs with an armful of preserving jars and landing among the several score that infested the cellar for half of every year before the freezer came.

The directions concerning what to freeze and what not to are so simple that a child of eight could understand them. One child of eight understood them so well that I recently thawed out a snowball under the impression that it was some badly-packaged white fish. My middle child was pained when she saw the pool of water and heard what I had done— she had shoved the snowball far down the freezer during a January storm, intending to use it as a teacher-flummox in July.

Non-freezables

You have to keep in mind that three categories of food should never be frozen under any circumstances. The first is highly individual, comprising any item that the family is unanimous in not liking, or the smell of which makes you quake when you have to cook it, or something which everybody likes, but only once in a twelvemonth.

However tempted you may be to snap up a cheap bulk bargain of fruit, fish, flesh, fowl or grain, if you don't like it don't buy it, and doubly don't freeze it. You won't like it any better when it has been frozen, and you won't be able to pass it off any more readily on your loved ones.

Whatever it is, it will descend by jerky stages to the bottom of the freezer, growing ever more out of date and bulking itself into valuable space until the day you hurl it into the dustbin with wild cries of remorse.

The second category is ordinary good sense. Do not on any account—not even with your fingers crossed and the famous last words on your lips 'Oh, it'll be *all right*', buy for the freezer or cook for the freezer any item or ingredient in less than prime condition.

The meat does not have to be steaming from the hoof, or the fish wriggling frantically, though this last might not be such a bad idea, but everything right down to the cooking fat and seasoning should be as fresh as, or fresher than, you would ordinarily use for immediate consumption.

This is what you have to remember—natural and irreversible processes of deterioration begin to set in the moment a beast is slaughtered, a fish hooked, a vegetable dug from the ground or a fruit picked from its bush. In fish, meat and most fruits, freezing only stops the process at the point it has already reached when the food is put into the freezer. In the case of vegetables, pre-freezing blanching destroys enzyme activity.

If you freeze a tough old piece of mutton, it will be no less old and not a scrap less tough when it is thawed and cooked. If you freeze a fly-blown fowl, you will get your own version of the rude old joke about the camel—chicken fly-blown, but beautifully frozen. If you freeze tired vegetables and exhausted fruit, they will lie just as wearily on the dish when you thaw them out six months later.

No method of preservation will make poor or old food good and fresh, not even freezing. You get out of the freezer exactly what you put into it, in more senses than one.

The third category of non-freezers is mandatory, having proved to be bad freezing material on technical grounds. Salad vegetables, lettuce and cucumber particularly, will not freeze–at least, they will *freeze*, but be unusable, limp and wet on thawing.

Raw potatoes fare badly, too, even if there were a good reason for freezing them, which there hardly is. Only the youngest and most beautiful home-grown specimens of root vegetables will repay the time and effort of freezing. Bananas freeze to brown mush, and should not be included in any made-up puddings or mixed fruit bags. Melons freeze well if cubed and packed in sugar syrup, with a little chopped preserved ginger if you like it.

Hard-boiled eggs will not keep even overnight in the freezer without going leathery and shrunken in the whites. This means that Scotch eggs should not be frozen, which is rather a pity, and neither should meat pies have hard-boiled eggs put down the middle of the filling.

Bottled or home-made mayonnaise will not freeze satisfactorily, either. Experts have tried every combination of olive oil, salad oil, wine vinegar and malt, lemon juice and dashes of hot water in attempts to make a freezable mayonnaise, but it never comes out of the freezer looking any more pleasing than leftover wallpaper paste. The taste is similar, too.

Short-term freezer foods

Any meat or fish that has been subjected to a curing process should not be kept in the freezer for more than a few weeks. This includes ham and bacon, in rashers or slices or even included in a pie or casserole, also kippers or bloaters.

The high salt content of cured food brings about the acceleration of oxidation and turns salted meat rancid more quickly than unsalted. It won't be bad in the sense of being injurious to health, but it will smell and taste most unpleasant. Bacon *can* be put into the freezer, though it is as well off in the refrigerator. If raw bacon is frozen its fat may develop a pink colour but this disappears during cooking and the flavour is not impaired. Rashers of bacon, like meat chops, should be interleaved with polythene so that they can be separated straight from the freezer.

If a dish demands rolls or snippets of bacon or ham, they can be cooked before freezing but the freezer life of the food will be reduced. If you intend keeping a dish for several months, add cooked pieces of bacon during reheating.

Meat with a thick layer of fat—belly pork, brisket, breast of lamb—is better used at once than frozen. Fat becomes rancid in too short a time to make it a good freezer item in the sense of being economical in the long term.

Freezer questionables Milk will not always freeze successfully unless homogenized and single cream (18% butter fat) always separates. Double cream (with 48%) and whipping cream (38% butter fat) freeze well when whipped. If they are frozen without prior whipping, they may separate and become unacceptably granular, but the higher the butter fat content, the better the chance of success. The addition of sugar before freezing helps to retain smooth texture. One tablespoon of sugar to $\frac{1}{4}$ pint double cream give a good texture, but this is so sweet it is best used in made up dishes, such as soufflés, rather than as an accompaniment to fruit.

Emulsion-based sauce mixtures, like mayonnaise or hollandaise, separate in the freezer. Butter-cream cake fillings will survive by virtue of having a high sugar content. They will survive even better if luxury margarine is used instead of butter. In fact, margarine is the product of choice for freezer cooking—the only drawback being that anybody who remembers longing for a big lump of butter throughout the war years can never regard marge as anything but a regrettable substitute. This is just something you have to fight down. It doesn't hold good any more.

The same applies to dried milk. Kicking and screaming, one had to drink National Dried for breakfast when the milkman had been kept up too late on fire-watching to bring the daily half-pint. The contemporary version wouldn't acknowledge the greyish fluid of yesteryear. However searing your childhood memories, you should still consider dried skim milk rather than fresh in making cream soup or sauce for freezing. The cream proper can be stirred in during reheating.

Cake icing is one of the very few 'freezer questionables'. Glacé, royal, fondant or what you will, are sometimes successful but may crack across the surface and lift clear of the cake, leaving you with a bald confection in one hand and a prettily-iced polythene bag in the other. It helps to freeze and

28

store the cakes in a polythene box or tin. To be sure of success ice the cake during its thawing time—the cold surface will set glacé or fondant icing in time to look well on the table.

Some old wives' tales   A further category of food includes everything that 'they' have always said can't be frozen successfully and perfectly well can. Plain or flavoured white sauce made by the usual roux method with margarine, plain flour and reconstituted dried skim milk will freeze—though it will probably have to be beaten briskly during reheating to curb any tendency towards separation. Do not substitute cornflour for the flour because you will end up with a gelatinous, unappetizing mass.

Mushrooms will freeze and not end up all mush and no room, if they are first sliced and sautéed in margarine. If you pick, grow or are given a large quantity of fine mushrooms, it is worthwhile heating a deep frying pan of vegetable oil and dunking the delectable fungus for a few seconds. Drain carefully before freezing in waxed or plastic containers, and the mushrooms can be used with the breakfast bacon or included in a made-up dish, in soup or as filling for an omelette.

It has been axiomatic up till now that you shouldn't freeze rice, pasta or pulses—they were alleged to sink into squelching oblivion. They do not in fact behave in this way and can be frozen successfully. But pasta takes so long to thaw that you could have cooked a ton of spaghetti in the same time. Rice, cooked in the usual way, does justify its place in the freezer. The grains can be separated after thawing, spread on a plate and warmed in the oven in only 10–15 minutes.

Perfectly drained, dry, cooked rice will keep for months in a polythene bag in the freezer. Macaroni and spaghetti are best not frozen. The dried pasta can be cooked while an appropriate sauce from the freezer is heated.

The pulses—butter and haricot beans, split peas and lentils—with their long soaking and cooking time, are wondrously useful extra-vegetable or soup-addition emergency supplies to hold cooked and ready for serving. They should be *just* cooked—not beginning to break up—before packing gently to avoid damage and freezing in cartons.

With this much said, there is nothing else in the realm of cookery from the humblest to the most haute that cannot be frozen and stored in a home freezer, as long as its origins are acceptable—and more of this in the next chapter.

From here onwards, you are guided in what you freeze by your own palate, purse and inclinations. It is clever to keep in your freezer as much soft summer fruit as you can afford and make space for.

Fruits for freezing　　Apricots, raspberries, strawberries, black- and red-currants loganberries, gooseberries and cherries, most fruits in fact, keep from one season to the next in sound condition.

Freezing soft fruits with sugar or syrup is not always a good idea unless you intend to serve them stewed or made into pies—they will be very soft on thawing. Frozen 'dry', with no more attention than picking over to weed out any marked specimens—they are taken out of the freezer about eight hours ahead of eating time and left in their pack in the refrigerator. Cherries, apricots, pears, gooseberries, plums and rhubarb benefit from being frozen in sugar syrup.

Fruit pies can be frozen cooked or raw. Raw pies are preferable partly because the pastry is actually improved by freezing, partly because you don't know you have been clumsy and squashed the cooked pastry until it's too late. One or two cooked pies only, for rapid serving, will save teeth-gnashing at a later date.

The same principle applies to meat pies. Steak and kidney pies ready for cooking can be made in normal-size dishes, but pork, veal or mutton pies for eating cold should be cooked in individual foil dishes.

Freeze what you like　　A home freezer will hold meat, soup, stock, sauces, steamed puddings either cooked or mixed ready for cooking in foil basins, batter, buns, sponge cakes, bread and bread dough, surplus eggs lightly beaten with a pinch of salt or sugar and carefully labelled as to number and 'addition', fruit that you can't be bothered to make into jam immediately, cake or biscuit mixes you haven't time to cook straight away, game and poultry, raw or cooked or made up into prepared dishes, very fresh fish, weighed-out quantities of raw pastry, meringues in plastic boxes, casseroles, stews and curries. If you like it, you freeze it.

Freezer life　　Keep a clear distinction in your mind, and in your freezer, about food for long and short-term storage. In general terms, keep fish and shellfish no longer than two to four months, meat sauces and pies no longer than four or five months, game no longer than two months, soup and stock six months, pork three months, beef, lamb and veal nine months, fruit and vegetables, bread and cakes up to a year.

In practice, nothing except soft fruit and seasonal vegetables, is ever kept in a home freezer longer than two or three months. The turnover in a household where three meals are eaten a day and parties given from time to time is quicker than you think.

The benefit of having frozen food to hand is in its very

immediacy, in being able to cook today, or when you feel like it, some dishes that you will want to eat next week when you won't have time for cooking.

The very long-term items are fringe benefits in that they are obtainable only for a limited time each year.

The reason for remaining within time limits is to maintain what the trade calls 'high quality life'. If you exceed the time limit on any particular item by too great a margin, the food will remain perfectly safe to eat, but its flavour and colour will gradually deteriorate.

Space-saving

It is also useful to remember that your freezer is far from bottomless, however large it may be. It is bad economy to use space on fruit and vegetables which are readily available to a town household at a consistent price all the year round.

This cuts out cabbage, all the root vegetables except sweet little beetroots and baby carrots pulled at finger-length in June, apples and pears for eating raw, oranges and bananas.

A remote country house is a slightly different case, but even the farthest rustic is not very likely to be snowed up for long enough to see the potatoes and swedes mouldering in the vegetable rack.

Anyway, the marooned would be far better consoled by having something deliciously out of season to eat in front of their cardboard-box burning fire.

For this same reason, I think it unreasonable to fill a small town-house freezer, at least, with home-frozen peas, sliced beans, potato chips, or anything else in the non-luxury class which can easily be bought commercially frozen in two- or three-pound bags—and at reduced prices at that.

A really hard-working home freezer contains nothing but items beloved of all, as much as possible of the goods which are madly expensive for forty-eight weeks of every year and maddeningly attainable for the odd four, as well as a supply of staple food.

This variety should cover enough complete meals or the components thereof to cover every thinkable and unthinkable emergency, from the arrival of a mad aunt at midnight to the descent of an American friend with five children at two hours' notice on an early-closing day—when I endured this shattering experience, those children didn't even wait for the food to *thaw*, which says something rather revealing about the transatlantic way of life.

Use a good third of the freezer for cooked food—casseroles, pies, stews and soup are the real life-savers, with soft fruit, bread, pastry and cakes coming up close behind.

Refreezing food

Retain leftovers of meat and poultry in the freezer for the dead end of the housekeeping week rather than handing them out on Monday. It is exactly this kind of thing that makes the anti-freezers close their eyes and shake.

If you remember, frozen food wrappings used to carry a big-print warning about not refreezing after thawing. So many people came to believe quite wrongly that this meant the practice was inevitably dangerous that the caution is not widely used any more.

All it really meant was that refrozen food would not have the quality of flavour, colour and texture that the conscientious freezing firms thought desirable for their customers' palates and their own reputations.

In fact and in practice, you can refreeze raw food which has not thawed completely if you are so inclined and refreezing food after cooking is perfectly in order. This will happen if you thaw a chicken to make a *poulet á l'estragon* and freeze the completed dish. If you then refreeze the remains of the dish, cool it rapidly and do not allow it to stand at room temperature before freezing, it may have lost its first fine careless rapture of taste, but you won't come to harm from it.

5 Shopping Around

Everybody goes shopping like fury when they begin to live with a home freezer. It must be something to do with the shock of opening up for the first time and gazing into a veritable pit, so clean, dark and empty.

It comes as an affront to one's domestic competence, like a bread bin with nothing in it but a forgotten crust crouching in a nest of furry greenery. It also gives one a nervous twinge, a feeling of 'whatever have I done?'

You can't imagine your budget ever stretching far enough to fill such a terrifying maw, and as for cooking enough dainty dishes to come even half-way up . . . So you find yourself scuttling about the supermarket, looking for things to freeze.

Don't try to fight this very natural reaction. As kind grandmas say to little boys being sick all over the Aubusson: 'It's better out than in.' It's better that you should find out quickly, in one violent episode, that shopping for the freezer isn't just a matter of bulk purchase for its own sake, nor even for the sake of the discount.

Budgeting Rather is it a matter of adjusting your system of marketing according to the season of the year instead of the day of the week. You have room for greater selectivity once you are free of gloomy obligations like brussels sprouts and turnips all the way from November to March.

After a few possible falls into the red, your budget grows supple enough to cope with a heavy seasonal shopping load and regain its strength during the lean times—lean times for everybody else, that is.

When others are paying dearly for their vegetables, you are enjoying haricots verts and sweet green peas. You don't even have to go out for them, either.

And when others are getting rashes from trying to make the

33

most of the few weeks when the strawberries have recovered from the conditions that the growers annually declare have decimated the crop, you are able to relish the glut and have the pleasing thought of strawberries and cream on Boxing Day to boot.

Unless you are constitutionally addicted to keeping bills for years and staying up late at night to find out why your change was a few pence on the wrong side, you will not be affected by the altered method of budgeting.

It just happens over a year. The thin spending weeks balance the fat ones without your having done much about it—unless you get carried away in a thin week and spend the float on frivolity. This is a very real danger to those of us who are accustomed to seeing nothing but bits of fluff in the housekeeping purse between Tuesday and Friday. Good managers will not fall into this error, but others should be on their guard.

Shopping list

The changed pattern of shopping does, however, require forethought and a measure of trial and error to find a pattern to suit your own circumstances and freezer capacity. For the very first time, it becomes possible *really* to shop only once a week, and to reduce the regular week-end weight-lifting exercises down to a single shopping basket.

I had a friend who was rather tediously proud of her shopping ability—'Never more than once a week, dear, two hours every Friday morning and that's the *lot.*' Having dined with her on a Thursday night, and listened to her husband's indigestion, it took me some considerable time to break my own resolve to shop twice a day if that were the only way to avoid such a gruesome régime.

Without a freezer to back you up, weekly shopping is either a big lie or not caring what you eat from Tuesday onwards. *With* a freezer, the weekly shop can be reduced to potatoes, hard fruit, leaf and salad vegetables and dry goods. Everything else, if the circumstances are favourable, can be bought at much longer intervals.

The daily pestilence of bread buying, or bread forgetting, is banished for ever. At one fell swoop you can buy as much cut bread, loaves or rolls as your freezer capacity will reasonably permit. You can buy currant buns, crumpets, sponge cakes, scones, just as the spirit moves—all the bakery goods that stale overnight in the cake tin have a freezer life of months and should be bought or made on the same basis as the bread.

The worthy mousetrap cheese is cheap when unmatured,

34

but rather lacking in tang. If you can afford space for a seven- or even ten-pound wedge, cut it into convenient and well-wrapped pieces and it will mature splendidly during its freezer life.

You can buy vacuum-packed bacon rashers to keep in the freezer for six weeks. This is worth doing if you can buy the rashers in wholesale quantity and show a saving over shop prices, and if your normal consumption of bacon is great enough to warrant the outlay.

Bulk buying in tins

If you can buy giant-sized super-economy cans of fruit, fruit and vegetable juices, frankfurters, skinless sausages, even baked beans, they can be opened and divided into suitable portions. This may not be a very sophisticated use of the freezer, but it is severely practical if you have enough freezer capacity and a family with a penchant for things on toast late at night, or snacks after school. The texture of these foods may suffer somewhat, but if they are normally to be eaten frequently it would be worth freezing some canned foods.

The main shopping difference comes about in being able to buy and store commercially-frozen food in quantity. Let us be frank—nobody who lives in a town and hasn't a garden is going to bother with freezing any vegetables other than the most rare and luxurious, or those brought in leaf-lined baskets by country friends who feel they are doing good to the underprivileged.

And nobody who dislikes cooking or can't find the time for anything but the most basic boiling, is going to give a thought to her problems of puddings, cakes, pies or pastry when she can buy a case of this and a dozen of that and six individual servings of the other.

This change operates in two ways—you don't have to go out and haul the stuff home, for one thing. Even allowing for the hair-raising price rises that Our Betters say are not as steep as we very well know they *are*, you know to the last penny what a month's supply of your chosen food is going to cost at catalogued prices. Seasonal variations in prices don't apply at all, which is more than you can imagine happening in the market place.

The last two or three years have seen the bulk-supply side of the frozen food industry expand into the domestic market as never before, and it will be a continuing trend. Bulk buying is always more economical than buying in small quantities for day-to-day needs. A freezer enables you to buy commercially-frozen food in large quantities at a real saving.

The Birds Eye Freezer Service

And by using the Birds Eye Home Freezer Service you are assured of receiving guaranteed top quality food.

There is a large variety of frozen foods available. In all there are over a hundred items from which to choose—everything from garden peas to scampi, from orange juice to Dover sole. And all at very special prices.

Here's the drill:

1. Phone your nearest Birds Eye depot for a price list and details of the free delivery service in your area.

2. Choose the products you want from an extensive range and phone in your order.

3. All deliveries are made in refrigerated vans.

4. The minimum order value is only £5 and payment is by cash on delivery.

I have known people to take fright at the idea of putting out a straight fiver, or even more, on a single order of frozen food. This is the attitude of those geared to the idea of eight-ounce packets of beans, small bags of chips, fish fingers in packets of ten, and ice-cream in 'Family Bricks'. It is not the attitude of the home-freezer owner, who aims for higher things.

Buying little frozen packs means spending more to buy less over a long period. Buying in bulk means spending less to buy more at long intervals, or it can mean spending the same amount of money on food but having a much more interesting and varied menu.

The annual saving represented by even a small indulgence in bulk buying—and most firms list anything up to 100 different items—will go a long way towards recovering the outlay on a home freezer in its first two or three years of working.

If there *is* a snare in bulk buying, it is the sneaky one of finding yourself dazzled by your own rich store. Not seeing quite straight, and being accustomed to short-term shopping, you hurl the delicacies about like there was no tomorrow.

Be firm with yourself. It isn't that the salesman will wonder about you when you have to telephone another order a fortnight after the first, but the advantages of convenience and economy are lost if you consume the stuff in an unconsidered fashion simply because it's *there*.

To avoid this failing, be sure that you are supplied with vegetables anyway in free-running packs, in which the vegetables are loose, not solid packs where they are stuck together. Whacking a piece off in the kitchen is the certain way to cook more than you need. Cut a big corner off a free-running pack and *measure* your requirements into the pan.

Bulk suppliers

If you buy in bulk from any of the great national frozen food firms, you will not have any problems of quality, variety or standards of service. But over the past two or three years, private firms have been entering the frozen food market here and there. Butchers, particularly, have seen a way of extending their enterprises. Others have started up from scratch as direct suppliers of frozen food for home freezers.

I think it is only prudent to treat these suppliers exactly as you treat any new butcher, greengrocer or provision merchant who opens shop in the district. This is to say that you wait until somebody else has tried and proved them, rather than offering yourself as a test case. Obviously, the unfortunate dealers would never get off the floor if everybody followed this policy, but everybody won't.

It is usually a private firm which will offer to stock a freezer hired from them at rates varying according to the size of freezer—from about 50p a month for a four cubic foot up to £3 or more for a twelve or fourteen cubic foot size. At these rates, you are a long time in showing any real economy in frozen food, because the hire charge counters the lower prices.

A freezer of your own from the beginning is the best idea, unless you dislike tying up a capital sum, or can't manage the whole outlay, or are constantly moving house and having to empty the freezer each time.

When you begin to shop for goods for your freezer, view the entire commercial bulk field and do not bestow your custom on the first person to solicit it. Just remember the priorities—quality, price, variety, and reliability both in delivery times and trading status. The very last thing you want is to have your supplier going out of business, for whatever reason, with either your capital or your catering involved in his affairs.

Whether you deal with a national or local firm for bulk delivery, you will still be offered almost exclusively the products of the big organizations, because it takes corporation-sized resources to set up and operate freezing plants.

Meat from the bulk supplier

What a private firm *will* offer on its own account is meat in whole carcasses, sides, half sides and prepared packs of smaller joints, chops, steaks and mince, as well as poultry whole or jointed.

And this, unfortunately, is exactly the field in which the

freezer owner can come to the most horrible grief if anything goes amiss, whoever her dealer may be.

The stuff of nightmares lies in having bought 56 lb. of 'best beef', which will cost upwards of £15, and finding out after the first cut that it isn't any such thing. You could take it back and throw it at the supplier, but you might be charged with assault and the fine would add to the butcher's bill.

Meat looks at first sight to be the best freezer bet for anybody—but I think the rule doesn't apply to *everybody*. It certainly applies to homes with large freezers and housekeepers who can afford to invest heavily in one commodity, to farmers, far-flung country dwellers, caterers and people with uncles who run butcher's shops.

But for town dwellers, families with not-very-elastic budgets or small freezers used mostly as background food storage—think not twice but many times before deciding on a bulk purchase of meat.

If you buy a large quantity of meat already butchered, packed and frozen, you need courage, money and ample freezer space. Courage is necessary to look the supplier in the eye and demand to be sold a sample of his meat before any irrevocable decision is taken. If he won't oblige, call off the deal. You don't want to play Russian Roulette with half a side of beef.

If you attempt a mass purchase of fresh meat at wholesale price, you may well have to butcher it yourself or accept the quite considerable charge for having the job done in the shop. The butcher has to live, poor man, and when you have once tried to joint a huge carcass, encountering the astonishing resistance that even a stone-dead sheep can put up against interference with its person, you will be more charitably disposed towards butchers for evermore.

Even when you have wrestled the corpse to pieces—one can seldom put the process on a higher plane than that—the freezing of forty or fifty pounds of meat will have to be spread over at least three days in a freezer of much less than twelve cubic foot capacity.

I don't even feel quite certain that the ten or twelve per cent price saving is always justified. If you are offered carcass beef at something like 30p a pound *overall*, or lamb at about 18p, you are certainly getting a good bargain in fillet steak or chump chops.

But you are paying at the same rate for the lower-priced cuts, the scrag end, the brisket, the breast of lamb and the shin of beef. You are even paying for the inevitable nasty,

◄ Orange soufflé made with frozen concentrated orange juice, frozen egg whites and whipping cream. It is decorated with frozen cream and peel cut from an orange

1
A sponge flan from the freezer, filled with frozen fruit and decorated with whipped cream

2
Assorted fruits being prepared for freezing in syrup

3
Currants, raspberries and slices of bread from the freezer make a summer pudding which is a special treat in mid-winter

4
This rhubarb crumble was made with rhubarb frozen in syrup, and a frozen rubbed-in mixture

1

2

3

4

horny bits that make everybody go 'Yuk!' and have to be fed to the cat.

There is no need to be deterred absolutely by these darkling observations. They are offered as a means of cushioning you against any rude shocks you might otherwise have suffered in the meat market.

If you consider them only in the light of your own circumstances you will be able to decide whether you and your freezer have the required qualities of determination and space.

But I would suggest that if you are in the proud position of knowing a butcher who sells only meat of most impeccable quality *all the time*, and if this admirable tradesman will supply you regularly with joints and cuts of your own choice in a quantity to suit your own purse and freezing capacity, this is a happy compromise.

You may not effect such startling economies, but you will be shopping for the freezer in a way that makes the best sense —for the sheer, blissful convenience of having good food to hand when you want it.

Poultry purchases   The number of chickens, ducks, turkeys—frozen or otherwise—that you buy at any one time is dictated by freezer capacity almost as much as price, and convenience as much as either. It *is* very convenient, it should be pointed out, to buy a turkey just before the Christmas rush and price rise, or just after to provide an Easter splendour.

It is less provident to buy poultry in quantity than game. Chicken is always available, but pheasant, grouse, pigeons, hare and even venison are limited in season. No game is ever exactly cheap, even if you buy it warm from the retriever, but there are regular periods when it is less dear than usual.

If the budget permits, invest in the species you like best at the most favourable price, and you will cover dinner-party possibilities for some months ahead.

While we are on the subject of flesh and fowl, I beg you to profit from the awful experience of the woman whose garden backs on to mine. She was offered 'a real snip' in meat by a man her father met in a pub—an excellent trading area in many respects, but not on this occasion.

That meat has never been properly identified to this day. I have always held that it was a greyhound, judging by its state of extreme emaciation and length of leg.

The moral is that bargain beasts and birds never *are* bargains, and should be spurned. If meat is cheap, there is likely to be good reason! That it might have been stolen is the least of the possibilities. One will go further and say that 'bargain' food of any kind is always suspect, and not to be confused with food bought at a comparatively low price in a seasonal glut.

It was with this in mind that I earlier used the words 'if the circumstances are favourable'. I meant the shopping circumstances—where you shop, when you shop, and from whom you shop. These factors are important to anybody shopping for food. To a freezer owner, shopping for a larger quantity of food than usual and requiring its condition to be better than average, they are of absolutely vital importance.

Fish for freezing

The circumstances of living far inland do not favour buying salt-water fish or shellfish for home freezing from a city fishmonger. Freshwater fish is fine if you live near a river, reservoir or lakeland, and if you know for *certain* that the shop has its own supplies brought freshly to the counter in each season.

This is no disrespect to the thousands of upright and worthy fishmongers who ply their trade a day's journey from the sea. Their kippers will make a king's breakfast and their plaice a noble tea, but in spite of every benefit of refrigerated vans and rail freighters, their wares are a long way from home. Fish, above all other creatures, was designed by divine intent to travel only by water—in it, not on it.

The idea of buying fish for home freezing only if you live within spitting distance of the open sea is in order to lay hands upon it in the very short space of time when it can be called truly 'fresh'.

Meat, game, poultry and many vegetables are acceptably 'fresh' after a period of days, in that their natural deterioration is not far enough advanced to be noticeable. In fish, this period is measured in hours.

The real trouble lies in the rapid autolysis that occurs in fish—the same process that renders meat and game tender during 'ageing' or hanging, but without the same desirable result. It is a breaking down of protein molecules through enzyme activity, a sort of misplaced digestive process which, allied to the relatively low acidity of a fish, all too quickly wrecks its flavour and texture and makes it not worth freezing.

Oily fish—herrings, halibut, sardines—become rancid faster even than fat meats.

The only possible circumstances for buying crabs and lobsters for freezing are either with the sound of the sea in your ears, or if they are frozen solid on the fishmonger's slab and you can get them into your own freezer in the same state. Bought like this, in season and not at the usual alarming price for the grander crustaceans, they are well worthwhile in spite of having a comparatively short span of satisfactory freezer life.

Unless you are inordinately fond of fish, salmon in its high season and *not* previously frozen is the only one worth the effort and expense of buying for the freezer. One annual purchase of a whole salmon, with the gleam of its last leap still on its scales, is a very uplifting experience.

Summer fruits and vegetables

The group of perishables which make the best home-freezing material as good long-term storage prospects and showing a real economy of purchase are soft fruit and summer vegetables, either home grown or those imported in quantity only for short periods every year.

The only thing to be avoided in buying raspberries, strawberries and currants for the freezer is buying too many and perhaps robbing them for ever of their marvellous summer-time mystique.

You need *just* enough to take you round to early spring of the following year, leaving a couple of months in which to work up a new hankering for the warm, rich smell of fruit from under the sun. Serve them with proper ceremony on birthdays, Boxing Day and when it snows, to visiting firemen of the first importance, to people convalescing from the flu, and to yourself when you feel you deserve nothing less.

Watch the circumstances of purchase, however. Don't buy squashy-looking fruit just because it's cheap, and buy in the first week of the full crop when the fruit is dry and firm, rather than in the last when the quality has dropped off and the berries are becoming watery.

Buy direct from a grower if you can, or speak firmly yet kindly to the greengrocer about your special requirements. If he doesn't voluntarily give a discount on a big purchase, speak more firmly and he probably will.

Imported peaches, apricots and nectarines are worth buying for the freezer in their short season under two favourable conditions—if you can spare freezer space as easily as cupboard space for the same thing in cans, and, if possible, first sample from the batch you propose to buy. Some of the yellow-fleshed Italian peaches are watery, but the pale-coloured French ones are a good freezer buy in the week or so when they are very cheap.

I still hold that *buying* peas, broad beans, stick and French beans, spinach, sweet corn or carrots from a town shop for home freezing is false economy. They are not likely to be less than two days old, allowing for time taken in transport from

41

the grower to the wholesaler, in being packed and arriving at the shop. Their quality will probably be appreciably below the level required for satisfactory freezer results. And if you buy them at all, you buy enough to last almost round to the next season. For that length of time they will be occupying freezer space that you are pretty certain to wish you had free for something else at Christmas. It *would* be free if you bought vegetables in bulk packets at reasonable intervals through the winter months.

Buying a quantity of freshly picked summer vegetables at a farm gate is a different thing, and eminently desirable if the price is right and you are quite sure they will be making the best use of freezer space. Growing them yourself is even more desirable, but that doesn't count as shopping.

Buy for freezing only those vegetables which are not available in commercial packs, or seldom found anywhere but at source in the countryside.

Stringless beans come into this category, lovely crisp little-finger length pods that are only topped and tailed before cooking, and the astonishing blue chinese beans that turn green in boiling water and taste of butter. Kohlrabi, too, with its indescribably delicate flavour, never gets as far as a shop without falling into a coma from which it never recovers. And if you can but find somebody who grows calabrese, the pale green Italian form of broccoli, buy it and freeze it and be glad.

Marrow is only worth freezing if it is a great favourite with all the family. I tend to think of marrows as being for Harvest Festivals and gardeners under the age of ten who like to have something *large* to show for their efforts. A seasonal purchase of courgettes is a different matter.

The price of these civilized forms of the dropsical marrow reaches its lowest point in later summer, conveniently at the same time as the biggest imports of green peppers and aubergines.

From the aspects of both money and space, you can well afford to buy a fair quantity of all of them. They will freeze compactly in slices and are vital for the pickling season, which you can postpone until school goes back by freezing the required amount to await your convenience. They are also the most obliging of extra vegetables served by themselves or in cooked dishes through the winter.

At the same time of the year, you have to decide whether you are going to buy tomatoes for the freezer. If you have ample space, you will probably show a saving by freezing sliced tomatoes and using them instead of the canned variety in winter cooking. They will be soft on thawing, and not suitable for salads or as a garnish. If you are going to be pressed for space, buy tomatoes only when the price is at rock bottom and the quality still good enough for making and freezing soup or purée, or preferably both.

In the final analysis your methods of shopping for the freezer will be determined by whether you are a town or country dweller, a good manager or a bad one, an active cook or a passive user of somebody else's efforts, but mostly by the increasing confidence that comes with experience.

Exactly what to buy, where to buy it, how much to pay for it and what quantity to buy, you will do in your second year of freezing without remembering how violently you twitched and twittered that first time.

6 The Good Plain Cook

A home freezer is a passive object, a more wholly obliging device than any other domestic appliance. It undertakes its duties rather in the manner of a conscientious clergyman, as much mindful of time to come as of time present. It never acts in a precipitate fashion.

A freezer makes few demands upon its owner beyond a supply of electricity for its motor, and gives due notice of its rare ailments so they may be cured before a chronic condition sets in.

I have good reasons for offering this eulogy on the species before saying a word about cooking for the home freezer. The first reason is a friend of mine, a woman of some character and by no means faint-hearted, who was in two minds about buying a freezer. As a devotee of the cult, I invited her to view my long-term stocks of food in the downstairs freezer.

Feeling really rather well satisfied with what I had to display, I went through the list. 'I make twenty pounds of ratatouille every year,' said I. 'And there's a gallon of tomato purée in those little cartons, and here's the pastry. I make seven pounds of that at a time, and ...'

'Great heavens!' cried my friend, going upstairs as quickly as she could. 'As if I haven't troubles enough, now you want me to set up in the mass-catering business. I'd have to stay up all *night*!'

That experience taught me the foolishness of leaping into a discourse on freezer cooking—it is as unnerving to the listener as telling an expectant mother how to handle teenage rebellion. It will be too late for her to change her mind about the whole exercise, but a potential freezer owner will be sent half-way back to burying food in casks of salt.

The other reason for going slowly is the potential mightiness of the freezer cooking field. Its horizons are vast and far, its surface still practically unscratched, and its possibilities pretty well unlimited.

It demands of a cook not new skills, but the extension of ordinary practical capabilities. Certainly, it requires more forethought than day-by-day cooking of family meals and a broader outlook on catering than the routine of joint today, cold meat tomorrow and mince on Tuesday.

What you like when you like

But cooking in quantity for the freezer gives variety and availability to prepared, home-cooked food in direct and gratifying ratio to the amount of effort expended—not always the case when you have laboured long over a one-shot meal which is no more than a lovely memory and a pile of washing-up within the hour.

Yet while the undertaking can look awesome when set into so many words, there is nowhere any element of compulsion to do a single thing about it. You can use a freezer for years and never deliberately cook a dish for freezing, never approach the thing with a home-cooked product except perhaps when you have prepared for dinner guests who tele-phone to say they are snowed up or in quarantine and can they come next week.

If we start with the premise that freezer cooking is a stimulus to the keen cook and a merciful release for the stressful, after-work chop griller, there is less chance of your turning pale and wondering about your chances of giving up domesticity for ever.

If we assume that nobody will want to freeze everything they *could* freeze, but most people will want to freeze *something*, the field of activity can be widely covered without precipitating any nervous crises.

We should begin at the very beginning, then, with plain cooking. And the very beginning of that lifelong commit-ment, which is implicit with all else in the promises about 'for better, for worse', is the prospect of providing at least two, probably three and maybe even four meals every day as long as ye both shall live.

And meals for not only ye both, but for all ensuing progeny as well. This is to say nothing of little friends to tea, fat friends to dinner, dieting relations for week-ends and vegetarian relations for Christmas—but let us leave them for the next chapter.

The fact is that when you have a home, you are going to be obliged to cook. When you have children, you are going to be obliged to cook a lot more. But when you have a freezer, you have the means of condensing the time spent on the preparation of meals from a number of intermittent hours every day to a single period of selected time.

If the preparation of a single dish or item is going to involve a dozen separate activities of hand and judgement, and six or more pieces of equipment are going to be handled, it is in every way desirable that the activity and equipment should be put to maximum use. In short, you might as well cook by the gallon as by the gill, because the *associated effort* on your part will be just about the same.

The preparation of food takes more time than either cooking or serving. It involves gathering ingredients, utensils and implements, going through the several processes of peeling, washing, cutting, measuring, mixing, stirring and standing that are involved in assembling a dish or a meal, and finally the washing and putting away of all the pots, pans, cutlery, bowls and boards, the cleaning of the stove, the wiping down of the working surfaces and the disposal of the peelings.

After a few years of domesticity, one goes through this relentless performance with the mind half-shut—if one gave it too much cool consideration too often, one would soon be taken away in a state of complete nervous decay.

Consider it coolly now. It gives the full answer to any tremors you may have about cooking for more—much, much more—than the next meal and a half.

Cooking equipment

It will also help you to be calm about the next step—equipping yourself to best advantage for freezer cooking. No particular piece of equipment is absolutely vital to success—if you cook in a tin pan on an oil stove you will get on beautifully just as you are, as long as there is an electric point for the freezer—but there is no need to be spartan if you can contrive otherwise.

If you are setting up home for the first time, or moving house, or rejuvenating a kitchen you're effectively stuck with, it would be a heaven-sent opportunity for thinking ahead in terms of freezer cooking.

Apart from being a chance to plan a freezer into position instead of having to wedge it in later with a jemmy, it would be the time to choose a large cooker with an oven big enough to hold two large casserole dishes or four eight-inch cake tins on one shelf. Cooking in quantity should save as much time as effort, but this will not work out as satisfactorily if you prepare in bulk but have to cook in batches.

This is a counsel of perfection, of course. Some of us make

do with the same kitchen appliances for life but some people have to be lucky sometimes. Those who are not lucky on a big scale can still make minor improvements.

It helps to have a multi-speed electric mixer with a large and a small bowl, a pressure cooker, a couple of large-size stewing pots, a real stockpot to hold four gallons and some of the oven-glass casseroles guaranteed to withstand far extremes of temperature.

None of these is essential—only helpful. What I think *is* vital is an enormous mixing bowl of some sort. With such an aid, you can mix pastry or rubbed-in cake mixtures without the irritation of flour climbing the sides of the bowl and rushing up your sleeve. It is also most helpful to have good muscles on the stirring arm, but these develop proportionately to the amount of exercise you give them. You should just *see* mine. . . .

Family likes and dis-likes
When you begin to cook for the freezer, keep right in the front of your mind the rule outlined in a slightly different context in Chapter Three. That is, cook according to your family's likes and dislikes, bearing the latter even more firmly in your mind than the former. Though they will be less numerous, they will get you into the most trouble.

You may have a lot of apples and a lot of blackberries and pastry, but if nobody likes blackberry and apple tart at the best of times, it will avail you nothing to cook and freeze it. They still won't like it.

On the other hand, if half the family loves garlic and the rest go about pointedly opening windows whenever they scent the aromatic bulb you can easily get the better of them. Leave half the quantity of a dish unflavoured and serve it with a slight sneer. Flavour the rest with crushed garlic—or dill, rosemary, marjoram or fennel—before freezing, and keep it to be eaten when the non-believers are away. But re-member to label the portions appropriately, otherwise your cunning may rebound on you.

But in the main, plain cooking for the freezer divides into two interchangeable categories—commercially frozen food bought in packs or portions, supplementing home-prepared cooked dishes or home-frozen ingredients. The first object of the exercise is to hold permanently in stock enough food in sufficient variety to give a selection of instant meals.

In terms of plain cooking, as distinct from more elaborate activity, this doesn't mean cooking *exclusively* for the freezer. It means cooking your usual main dishes in three- or four-fold quantities, and freezing the excess for the next

47

three or four occasions on which you would anyway have that kind of meal.

Casseroles and stews

Casserole food is likely to be the basis of this kind of catering, or any dish which is normally a long time a-cooking. The only difference in approach is remembering not to include any of the few proscribed ingredients—like hard-boiled eggs or bacon, ham and pork if the dish is destined for long frozen storage. Until your eye is in, use your normal-size serving dish to measure freezing quantities from the mass, and freeze each dishful in a separate container. And until your taste buds are accustomed to freezer cooking, use seasonings sparingly.

Plain stewed steak and kidney should be cooked in vast quantity, because of its many applications. It stands confidently alone with creamed potatoes and commercially frozen or fresh vegetables, turns into a pie straight from the freezer, with a piece of frozen pastry clamped over the top— the high temperature needed to cook pastry heats the meat right through at the same time. Steak and gravy becomes shepherd's pie* with mashed potatoes browned on top on the same principle as the pastry. If you cool the meat quickly, by standing the cooking dish or pan in cold water, you can seal it into squares of raw pastry and freeze pasties to be cooked just before a supper or a picnic.

All kinds of stewed meat, from humble Irish to grand goulash or carbonnade,* is worth making for the freezer on two counts—the quantity means that a better flavour will develop in the cooking, and you won't have to make it again for *weeks*. The only thing to be avoided is the overcooking of any stew containing vegetables like potatoes, carrots, turnips—because they may become mushy or have a poor flavour on reheating.

This will not happen if the vegetables are added to the meat at a slightly later stage than if the stew were to be served directly, leaving them a trifle undercooked when the meat is tender.

Cool stews as quickly as possible after cooking, standing a tightly-lidded metal stewpot under a running cold-water tap, or decanting the contents of an earthenware casserole into a large saucepan and standing it in cold water. Skim off fat before packing for the freezer in plastic containers or foil-lined dishes.

When the food is to be eaten, the reheating time in a slow oven will exactly finish the vegetables. The time of reheating depends on the quantity in one dish—uncover it from time to time to check its progress, and don't keep it waiting if you can avoid it.

Any dish of kidneys* or sweetbreads* can be cooked and frozen, leaving any cream to be added at reheating. This should be done gently over a pan of hot water rather than by direct heat on a burner or in the oven, which may be altogether too drying for the meat to withstand without hardening.

Do not freeze uncooked liver which has already been frozen and thawed in the butcher's shop. Buy it frozen, by all means, but keep it that way until you are ready to cook it.

Seasoning

There are two schools of thought on how to season food cooked for the freezer—some say freezing emphasizes seasoning, some say it is diminished. I don't think one can generalize, because the flavour of meat and poultry particularly will vary and need adjustments at any time. But it is wise to under-season slightly before freezing and to taste before serving the reheated food, at least until you have made up your own mind on the seasoning question. I keep up my grandmother's habit of mixing a spoonful of dry mustard with thick gravy after cooking—and in my case, after thawing.

Chickens

When you cook chicken* or chickens with a view to freezing, it is often useful to casserole them whole with salt to bring out the flavour, half a dozen black peppercorns to add zest, a couple of onions and a stick of celery for the sake of their juices. After cooking, you choose whether to joint the birds or cut them tidily down the middle, wrap the pieces individually for freezing, reduce the stock somewhat, and freeze that in separate labelled containers.

You thus furnish yourself with a near-infinity of chicken dishes rather than several of the same kind, by serving them later on with whatever kind of sauce you happen to fancy. Their own frozen stock forms the basis of the sauce, or, free from the chore of cooking the bare bird, you may be in the mood to invent an entirely new one.

If you want to freeze a roasted chicken, you will probably have to take off the skin after freezing and before serving. There seems to be no way to prevent the skin from becoming wrinkled and sad, like a downtrodden washerwoman's fingers. Flouring and frying joints is the sure way to keep crisp skin on chicken that is to be served cold.

No poultry, meat or game should be frozen with stuffing *inside* it. The carcass prevents full heat reaching the concealed stuffing to cook it right through before the bird is done. Any undesirable microbes which may be present might be given

49

just the right warmth and time to gather strength for an attack.

Trimmings for meat dishes

It is a remote risk, but not worth taking. It is entirely eliminated by not stuffing the bird and by cooking it really thoroughly. This principle does not apply to stuffed herrings or cod cutlets with stuffing, provided the fish itself complies with the rigid standards of freshness already mentioned since there is not the same resistance of flesh and bone to heat penetration.

But with fowl, you can go no further than ramming stuffing under the loose skin at the front end. Otherwise, make and freeze stuffing or forcemeat balls separately, and cook them separately.

It is in any case convenient to have a bag of breadcrumbs always in the freezer. A whole loaf crumbed at a sitting spares one the irritation of having to get out the grater to prepare the few tablespoons that are all a recipe usually requires, to say nothing of the saving on skin and fingernails—graters seem to prefer operating on living flesh.

More time yet is saved by using a blender to crumb bread and chop parsley and lemon rind all at the same time—the parsley doesn't wrap itself round the blender blades if it goes in with the bread. Add suet, beaten egg and seasoning to a measured quantity of the frozen ingredients, and the stuffing is ready. The same applies to sage and onion stuffing—blend the breadcrumbs, sage leaves and cooked onions and freeze the mixture, mixing the whole lot with softened butter, egg and seasonings before use.

Well up among the other 'trimmings' that go into the freezer to save time and effort are Yorkshire puddings*. To go one further, it is useful to have frozen toad in the hole* in store. How nice it would be to find and strangle the wretch who so crudely named that sturdy dish. The sausages are frozen raw in the uncooked batter, and like the individual Yorkshires, the dish is cooked directly from the frozen state.

You *can* freeze boiled suet puddings* too, cooked and frozen in the same foil basin.

Savoury puddings

The advantage comes about here if you have a family of suet-pudding eaters and have to make the long-winded things with any regularity. Making them two at a time, one in the pan and one in the steamer on top, shows a saving of effort and fuel. To be fair, savoury suet pudding has something to be said for it if one or two fresh sage and/or thyme leaves are chopped and mixed with the dough.

Pease pudding* will freeze satisfactorily, hearty filler and keeper-out-of-cold that it is. The trick is to make a whole lot in one large pan and divide it into serving portions for the freezer in the indispensable foil bowls.

Plainly roasted sliced meat, whether beef, pork or lamb, is not in itself good freezer material. It turns defiantly dry, however carefully packed it may be. If you want to serve cold roast meat particularly, it is better cooked only a day ahead and kept overnight covered in the refrigerator.

Roasting joints

Roasting joints, especially poultry, should *not* be cooked straight from the freezer. A large joint such as a rib of beef or leg of lamb may need as much as three times the normal cooking time and the oven heat will not penetrate sufficiently to cook the centre of the joint. Similarly, chops and meat steaks *can* be cooked from the frozen state, but not under the usual quick heat. Start with gentle heat to thaw the meat, and only finish with a brisk flame. If you attempt to give them the usual short, sharp cooking to seal the juices, the meat may very well be cold and raw when the outside is done to a fine brown turn, and again texture is likely to suffer.

Leftovers

It is best to consider leftover roast meat as material for made-up dishes of mince, rissoles, shepherd's pie or inventions. The meat can be packed and frozen in cut-up cubes ready for its further preparation, or the dish promptly made and frozen.

Leftover fish that has originally passed all the freezer tests, or extra quantities of cooked fish purposely prepared, can be flaked and promptly turned into fish cakes or fish pie for freezing.

Promptly is the operative word for handling all and any leftovers destined for freezing. Never leave the cooked remains of *anything* at room temperature before freezing. If you haven't the time or can't be bothered to process it immediately, *put it in the freezer until you can.*

One quick and crafty way of rejuvenating leftover lamb and veal—pork, too, but for a shorter storage period—is to serve it originally with onion sauce, which will not give anybody cause for complaint. But afterwards, cut the meat into cubes, mix it well into the remaining sauce, and freeze the whole lot. Reheat the mixture in the oven with extra seasoning and a garnish of sliced tomatoes.

Beef or mutton should be deliberately left over for making moussaka*, a beautiful combination of layered meat, aubergines, and tomatoes, made, cooked, frozen and finally served in an oven-glass dish so that its visual beauty is unimpaired. No one could call *that* a leftover.

51

With a freezer used to this extent for meat dishes, it becomes good economic policy to depend quite heavily on commercially frozen vegetables as accompaniments. It represents a more balanced use of the freezer in terms of cost, convenience and *immediate* availability of a whole meal.

The application of a freezer beyond main meals and into a wider range of cooking depends entirely on your own capacity as a cook and your desire to please. If you have a job outside the home and quite enough to do in keeping the stomachs from rumbling and the dust from piling up on the picture rails, you may well not want to go beyond the meat and veg.

If you just don't like cooking, you can leave it at that and broaden your order for bulk packs to include something of everything in the range. But if you do like to cook, or think you might learn to like it, or feel you ought to even if you don't at this moment, a freezer will decide for you one way or the other.

You may well, like me, be much taken by the feeling of security offered by a freezer you have largely stocked by your own two hands. A lot of people who were children in the war have this feeling, and the under twenty-fives can never understand it.

But then, they were never told to look miserable in the grocer's shop, so the assistant's heart might be melted to the extent of putting an extra milligramme of cheese on the scales. . . .

Cheese

Cheese—now there's a useful freezer item for use in dishes like cauliflower cheese and macaroni cheese*. It is well to make enough white sauce and have enough grated cheese for half a dozen portions and freeze these in containers ready for adding to cooked cauliflower or freshly cooked macaroni. But try macaroni cheese Mrs. Beeton's way, with macaroni, grated cheese and white sauce in distinct layers, not in a heap like fallen whitewashed scaffolding poles.

White sauce

Basic white sauce* can be made in quantity for the freezer, ready for sweet or savoury dishes. Make it with sweetened milk for pouring on steamed puddings, but infuse the milk with a bay leaf, a slice of onion and some peppercorns for making onion or cheese sauce*. Pack in serving quantities in firm containers—the obliging margarine carton is fine—and label very clearly.

Stock

A good supply of home-made bone stock* means that soup, meat sauces and gravy need never have the distinctive taste that announces you have been using stock cubes *again*. To make four pints of jellied stock takes about ten minutes' actual work to wipe the bones, cut up the vegetables and measure the water, after which the pan is left to its own devices on a low heat for several hours.

Jellied stock is better for the freezer than a similarly large quantity of the thin kind from a chicken, for instance. Its water content has almost disappeared so it is a valuable space saver.

With a rich base like that, you can make an enormous quantity of meat sauce, ready to serve with pasta. A sauce made with minced meat, onions, tomato purée and stock, properly called a ragu*, should be made for the freezer with garlic, subject to the prevailing taste, ground black pepper and basil—and rather more stock than if you were making it for immediate use. This allows for the slightly drying effect of low temperature, and some reduction in reheating.

Apple sauce

You will feel bound to make apple sauce if there is even one fruitful tree in your back yard. A year's supply of this commodity is not the alarming prospect that it sounds. Although it's useful, you don't use as much of it in a year as you do of many other items. Just make it plainly or add a little sage and freeze for serving with pork. But make some more and flavour it with vanilla sugar and perhaps chopped almonds, grated lemon peel and a clove for serving with custard sauce or for making into a flan.

Pastry

You cannot know until you have tried it how gratifying it is to have a *lot* of frozen pastry in the freezer—and a lot is seven pounds prepared weight, or ten, or fourteen if you have that kind of determination and space.

After one purposeful hour of rubbing-in, mixing and rolling, you are free for weeks or months from the annoyance of having your nail varnish worked off or having to get up on Sunday morning in time to make and chill a tiddly little piece of pastry for a pie.

As a bonus, raw pastry actually improves with freezing— the heavy-handed can produce flaky pastry for the first time, and quite humble shortcrust rises in the oven like a lark from the meadow. Even with a freezer, puff pastry is time-consuming to make and is probably better purchased ready made and frozen.

It is a matter of choice whether you cut up the finished mountain of pastry into one- or two-pound slabs for freezing, or line it into foil plates for tarts, or put in the filling and freeze whole pies, or shape *vol-au-vent* cases.

Prepared cases and shapes are convenient, though liable to be knocked about unless you can pack them firmly for freezing in a rigid plastic box or biscuit tin. Slabs of pastry ready for rolling out are useful for making small jam or fruit tartlets, or putting over or into a bigger foil pie dish or plate than you can easily keep in the freezer.

The only course to avoid is freezing the whole lot in a single lump. You will never be able to hack a small quantity free of the mass.

Family puddings

Since puddings are time-consuming to make, which is at least one of the reasons why they seem to be going out of style, as well as their being against the current trend for thinness, they repay being made in freezer quantities. This applies particularly if you have hungry boys in the house, and even more if they bring in other hungry boys whose mothers have stopped making puddings.

Steamed sponge pudding* mixtures can be made in a basic bulk from eggs, sugar, butter and flour, and then hived off into foil basins for individual flavouring.

Cakes

The amount of everyday cakes you choose to make and put into the freezer depends on what quantities are normally eaten in your house, whether you feel your cakes are better than bought ones, and how much freezer space you want to involve with fairly fragile items.

With these factors determined, it still is not worth freezing rich fruit cakes which keep satisfactorily in tins. It may sometimes be useful to keep an uncooked rich mixture in the freezer if for reasons of a failed or full-up oven or shortage of time, it cannot be cooked at once. The frozen mixture will need marginally more cooking time to allow for the thawing-through.

The home-made cake choice for the freezer is best made from sponge or sandwich cakes, Madeira or light fruit cakes made by the blending method, doughnuts, fancy cakes and buns.

Doughnuts, previously cooked and frozen, then reheated in the warming drawer and rolled in sugar before serving, seem to make a deeper impression on children than much more fanciful offerings. Sandwich cakes can be frozen with a flavoured butter-cream filling, or with whipped cream and/or jam. Whipped double cream may go yellowish, but 38% butter fat whipping cream is very satisfactory.

Cakes are useful items to have as freezer stand-bys. With them at hand, one is rarely caught in the awful, one-down situation of having to proffer an apologetic-looking cut cake

54

◀ Chocolate, jam, syrup and lemon sponge puddings from the freezer, served with sweet sauces

1
A lemon meringue pie assembled using pastry and egg whites from the freezer with egg yolks and lemon

2
Chocolate ice-cream from the freezer served with pears

3
Slices of Arctic Roll served with frozen canned peaches and raspberry purée

4
Frozen meringues and strawberries make a strawberry meringue gâteau suitable for a special occasion

1

2

3

4

to a visiting in-law or domestic rival, which is quite a consideration, but remember that cakes do need an hour or so to thaw. And if ever there was a case to be made out for not making in quantities of ten what you can make by dozens, it lies in fiddling fairy cakes.

Sandwiches

It lies in sandwiches too. When you are called upon to make sandwiches for a picnic, a school outing or the Brownie party, make a loaf-load of the boring contrivances. Any familiar sandwich filling will freeze, except lettuce, tomato or cucumber, or sardines if they are likely to be left in the freezer for long. Chopped egg and salad cream sandwiches should not be frozen either but meat or fish paste, meat, chicken, cheese, Marmite, pâté or tongue are satisfactory. It is fortunate that sweet sandwiches have quite gone out of style—frozen fillings of jam or honey have a regrettably unappetizing appearance after freezing. Do wrap sandwiches tightly, especially the meat variety, to prevent them drying.

With sandwiches and cakes in the freezer, you have a respectable tea right there and waiting on the days when you come home too late/cross/tired to make anything and your dependants hang about, grizzling, until supper-time. But again remember that food needs time to thaw.

Bread

I have deliberately left bread* as the last item of plain cooking for the freezer. Making bread is a therapy for the soul as much as the provision of a staple food. The rhythmic kneading, the deeply satisfying pull of the dough against your hands as you shape it into loaves, the smell of it reaching every corner and making people stop to sniff in the street outside—bread has something special to offer.

It also has the quality of requiring to be made in reasonable quantity or not at all. Without a freezer the reasonable quantity soon goes stale and undoes all the good work of its creation by showing itself so fallible after all. So make and cook bread when your soul needs it, and shape it into plaits or cosy cottage loaves, or neat little rolls, and put into the freezer all you can't eat immediately. Thaw at room temperature for an hour or more, according to size, or speed the process in a warm oven or warming drawer.

You can also 'flash bake' the dough, killing the yeast and setting the loaf by giving it ten to twelve minutes in a very hot oven, cooling and freezing it immediately and completing the cooking in a moderate oven at a later date. Watch the oven temperature to make sure the middle of the bread is quite cooked but the crust not burned. By either of these devices, you can offer freshly-baked bread or rolls at breakfast—

supposing you rise early enough or breakfast late enough—or impress visitors with the smell of baking bread while they wait for tea to be served. It is possible to freeze completely uncooked dough after the second proving. But in this case it is best to allow the dough to thaw before cooking so that it is cooked through by the time the crust is browned. The volume of a loaf made in this way is likely to be reduced. I still think, however, that the effect upon one's outlook is less marked than doing the whole satisfying job at one time.

If you like crusty bread, brush the top of the loaves with slightly salted beaten egg before baking. If you prefer a soft crust, make the bread with milk instead of water. In the latter case when the loaves come out of the oven, brush them quite lavishly with lukewarm milk and leave them covered with a clean tea-towel for fifteen minutes. They will remain soft if thawed at room temperature rather than by the more intense heat of an oven.

And do you know where I acquired those two handy hints on home cooking for the freezer? I got them from that very same friend who once fled at the sight and prospect of my downstairs freezer. It got her in the end, of course.

7 Fancy Cooking

I have said more than once in these pages that the home freezer represents a domestic revolution. I am about to say it yet again, in respect of what a rather stolid cousin of mine—a connection by marriage only, I am happy to say—insists on calling 'fancy cooking'. She refers to herself as 'a plain cook', in which she is absolutely right in every sense, but her admission is none the less shameful for all that.

It may be sadly true that most of us must eat a good deal of mince in our time and rarely or never feast on quail. Similarly, we will expect to eat more meals at the kitchen table in a hurry than ever we will enjoy from polished mahogany by candlelight. This is life, unfortunately, but there is still no need to allow the boiled-potato philosophy to become a matter of pride. It is the coward's way out, the sloven's armour.

The unregenerate plain cooks use lack of time as the prime alibi for producing uninspired meals on almost every day except Christmas, birthdays and anniversaries. Then they use these joyful occasions to prove their point by falling exhausted over the festive table, having been cooking without pause for days and days.

Cooking for special occasions

A home freezer takes away the time alibi equally from those who use it wilfully and those who wish they could do otherwise. The revolutionary quality lies in the freezer's unique ability to bring 'fancy cooking' down from its precipice of frenzied effort made against the clock and set it calmly alongside the plainest boiling.

Plain cooking for the freezer requires little more than cooking and freezing as you go along your normal culinary paths. For fancy cooking, the trick is to cook when you can, when you want to, when you feel like it; to cook when everybody is out, when the baby is having a nap, when the pressures

57

are off and your spirit is as light as your hand needs to be.

I sympathize—oh, *how* I sympathize—with working mothers who will go to any lengths to avoid having people to dinner on Saturday night, or mounting any kind of celebratory meal, because they know full well that the main feature of the menu will be Hostess in a Stew.

It can look like sheer masochism to attempt the cooking of an elaborate meal when the preparations have to be fitted between family lunch and nursery tea, when there will be diversions to find some string to make a cross-bow, some glue for a broken dolls' house or sticking plaster for a cut, when infant disputes will have to be arbitrated every six minutes and eight hundred calls for shoelaces and buttons to be undone or done up in every hour.

Even if you can dispose of the family for a whole day, or some pieces of the several preceding days, there is a limit to the amount of pre-preparation that one meal will stand.

The usual outcome of trying to build a party single-handed in one frantic spurt—not only the food, but setting the table, arranging the flowers, polishing the glass, shaking out the chair covers to free the lost bits of Lego and pieces of mangled biscuit, putting to bed children who don't want to go—is an advanced state of nervous tension and still not having your eyelashes on when the guests arrive.

I say 'usual outcome', because it applies to me and most of those I gladly call friends—but not to all. There are some who can manage dinner for a dozen and finish knitting an Arran jersey *as well*. One goes from year to year in the fading hope of one day coming upon them doing something untoward, even if it should only be licking the spoon and putting it back in the gravy.

Planned parties

A home freezer makes an end for ever to most kinds of domestic trauma. It lowers the inevitably high gear of super-cooking to a regulated idle through three courses spread over a week, or a month, or half a year. Any kind of entertaining is covered more easily by using a freezer than by any other means short of going out to a restaurant.

If a freezer is really gainfully and guilefully employed, its owner can achieve the wonder of giving a very grand party at virtually no notice at all, and without cooking one single item from scratch. There is no describing how elevated one feels on occasions like that. The sensation of omnipotence probably compares quite favourably with any other of mankind's most significant achievements.

The burning scarlet fuss of Christmas cooking, an annual

58

torment one is obliged to pretend to enjoy like anything, is cut down to size by a freezer. The statutory obligations, sweet and savoury, are all undertaken between Guy Fawkes' day and the first Sunday in Advent, give or take a week or two.

But at the same time, the more elaborate the cooking you undertake, the firmer should be your plan for its eventual use. I have found in myself and others a tendency towards a strange meanness about actually thawing and *using* the more splendid concoctions.

It must be the same force at work that keeps a magnificent hat in its box 'because it needs the right occasion to wear it'. The hat will go out of style, and the frozen dish will lose its flavour, so this tendency should be resisted.

Cook as exactly as you can to the form of your life. If you entertain to a regular pattern, with quite formal dinners or supper parties, you are justified in making and freezing say, *coq au vin*, in quantity. It will be used in the normal course of events, rather than being put by for possible use if and when.

If you run to casual meals for droppers-in, or only give a party once a year, you will be better served by soups*, pâtés*, pizzas*, casseroles* and a few lush sweet dishes. These will leaven the daily bread, but not involve you in time, effort and expense that may not be properly justified.

The more costly and elaborate the dish, the more important it becomes to check the ingredients for possible non-freezers or short-term only items. This becomes second nature after a while. It is no bar to any particular dish, because the odd ingredient can almost always be added on reheating.

Although most of the more ambitious, and thus more expensive, freezer food will be made for entertaining or festivals, there is much to be said for keeping just a few special delicacies always at hand. A hard day or a brisk fight can often be dissolved into serenity by the timely offering of something rich and rare that demanded no preparation— during which time the whole horror might have boiled up even higher.

Fancy cooking is even more of a seasonal matter than plain, if only because the best freezer economies are wrought by buying or growing more fresh food in its own short season than you would be able to store if you had no freezer.

High summer fruit and game* are the prime examples, being without freezer hazards. Lobsters and salmon*, if the absolute rules about freshness can be observed without actually getting yourself wet in doing so, have a short but definite period of being relatively inexpensive. They have a limited freezer life, not much more than two months, but better a little salmon for a short while than much cod for a lifetime.

Luxury vegetables, shop-bought or home-grown, indigenous or imported, have a place within or beside luxury dishes and should be counted as fancy cooking for freezer purposes. These include aubergines, courgettes, peppers, artichokes, haricot verts, the rather unpleasantly-named wax beans, and mange-tout peas which are almost never seen in shops but will grow in back gardens.

By having this wider range of extravagant ingredients in stock, and by developing a talent—or at least a liking—for cooking to higher purpose than merely warding off malnutrition, the freezer revolution now proceeds as far as you care to carry it.

To take it a good long distance for a start, consider all the items you would like to eat 'if only there were time to make them'.

Soups

Consider, first, the range of cream and puréed soups that take more time *every time* than the humbler broths or— whisper it, please, the canned variety.

A selection of delicate soup prepared for the freezer in quantity is a considerable improvement on the old trick of watering the soup to make a meal go further. It provides for small appetites who don't want anything heavy, or large ones who don't know when to stop, and for all the occasions when you have to offer *something* and there isn't anything.

This kind of soup takes in such refinements as cream of lettuce or watercress, asparagus, spinach, leek, or Vichyssoise, right down to the sturdy cream of tomato.

The basic recipes need no adjustment for freezing, but the cream and egg yolks used for thickening in some cases are best worked into the mixture during reheating. There is a possibility that the cream might separate from the puréed vegetables and stock, or you might just leave the reheating soup in the pan for too long and accidentally boil it into scrambled eggs.

If you are a congenital forgetter of things on the stove, you might make a habit of reheating soup—or sauce—in a double-boiler or in a bowl over a pan of simmering water.

The heartier soups—minestrone, lentil, ox-tail, pea, or French onion soup to be poured over baked bread with cheese—mightily repay the effort of their construction every few weeks in winter. All fat should be skimmed off meat soup

60

during cooling and before freezing. The essential bacon for minestrone or pea soup is best cooked in a piece instead of pieces, and taken out of the pan before the soup is frozen. Its memory will linger on, but its form will not remain to turn rancid and spoil the soup.

To avoid any chance of an overcooked flavour developing in mixed vegetable soup after reheating, it is as well to watch the pot and remove it from the stove a few minutes before you would otherwise consider it ready.

Onions, root vegetables, celery and leek should still be slightly resistant to a prod from a fork.

Haricot beans should not be allowed even to start breaking up, in case they disintegrate altogether if kept waiting longer on the heat than you anticipate before serving.

If this sounds a daunting performance, remember that you will be doing it but once in a way, not every single time you intend to serve a bowl of soup. There are times when home freezing requires a very radical change of outlook on the whole catering scene.

Pâtés and terrines   Consider next the range of pâtés and terrines* of liver*, meat, poultry* or game*. Although their freezer life is short they are worth making if you like them. They are tedious to make, certainly, but in fact less so when you have a solid quantity of meat to handle and when you can make them at leisure rather than in awful haste.

A half-pound portion of chicken livers merely serves to make a nasty mess round the bowl, enough to put one right off. Two pounds gives one something to *bash*, or the blender something to bite on with a will. The work period is hardly extended, and is well justified by the *grande luxe* appearance of the finished product.

Children will often eat a not-too-highly-seasoned pâté with hot buttered toast, when they will make retching gestures at plain liver. And grown-ups accustomed only to restaurant pâté and plastic-type terrines will fairly glow at the home-made variety. Apart from either of these two groups, there is something very satisfying about handing round a true luxury as if it were cheese sandwiches.

You will probably find that this kind of pulverized or shredded meat requires more seasoning—for adult consumption, at least—when made for freezing rather than immediate serving.

Rock salt helps the best flavour to develop. Add some coarsely ground black peppercorns while the meat is grinding and their zest will be distributed most evenly. If you like

61

garlic try a little in the pâté, and a blade of mace should go into the mixture, whether the recipe says so or not.

Leave out the layer of clarified butter that recipes usually require to be poured over the top of pâté dishes. Its purpose is to seal in the flavour, and is unnecessary under freezer conditions. Anyway, the butter just may take on an undesirable tang even during the short period of recommended storage.

Terrine dishes of pressed meat should be without the lining and covering of ham or bacon slices, unless you are perfectly sure they will be out of the freezer and eaten within a month, which they probably will not be. The fat in the bacon will very quickly turn rancid and wreck the entire dish.

Be thoughtful, too, if you are using goose or pork. Skim or cut off all possible fat, and do not count on storing in the freezer for longer than a month or six weeks.

Pack pâté in rectangular dishes covered with a piece of foil and enclosed in a polythene bag. If you have no idea of what quantity you will want to serve eventually, for two people or ten, put it into a large rectangular dish or loaf tin and place in the freezer until very firm. Remove and cut through the mass at several differently-spaced intervals, putting a double piece of foil between slices. Overwrap the whole in foil and a polythene bag.

If you want to serve a little, you take out the required amount without untidying the rest by hacking at it. If the lot is needed at one time, push all the slices together again. The cuts will not be noticeable when the pâté has softened slightly. This is a more satisfactory way of dealing with pâté than freezing it in individual dishes, which always turn out to be too big or too little for their purpose.

Pack a terrine in a round or oval or rectangular cake or bread tin or in a pie-dish, and cut as if it were a cake, with foil between the slices.

This pre-cutting is something to consider every time you are preparing items for freezing which are going to be sliced anyway. It works with pissaladière*, an impressive, fiddling, time-consuming and utterly delicious relation to pizza, which I heartily recommend as a freezer stand-by special.

Pissaladières

Pissaladière is based on a large circle of enriched bread dough, covered with onions, garlic and seasoning previously seethed in oil almost to a purée, and garnished on thawing with anchovies and stoned black olives.

One pissaladière takes as long to make as three, and if I didn't have a freezer I should yearn for it and wail about *time*.

But having a freezer, I have often produced slices of my secret weapon for people cringing at the prospect of little dead things on toast with their drinks.

It also comes straight out of the freezer to be garnished and thaw itself on the way to a better-than-average picnic, as well as providing a redolent Saturday lunch with a tomato salad and undressed lettuce. Not a nursery meal, by any means, but my goodness. . . .

Pizzas

Even the ordinary pizza*—ordinary by comparison, anyway—makes people go 'ooh!' and 'aah!' and tell their friends what a fine table you keep. This is only because pizzas are rarely made at home in this country. The delicatessen varieties often look as if somebody has just got up from sitting on them, and nearly always contain too many dried herbs.

But the home-made variety are splendid freezer stand-bys, and worth making by the half-dozen whenever you have the dough-kneading urge. They are a good starter to a meal, or a savoury if the main dish was light, or served instead of bread or rolls with a soup and salad supper—all you have to make at the time is the salad, if your cards have been played aright in the soup department.

When you arrive at the stage of preparing main dishes for the freezer, probably party dishes for the most part, you have no problem about where to start—only about where to stop. However, even the keenest freezer cook is going to be hobbled by her purse strings eventually, so let us proceed with that in mind.

The food that *ought* to be cooked for the freezer, as opposed to that which *might* be, revolves round dishes which take a long time to prepare and a long time to cook, and those comprising or containing items that must be seized in their due season.

'Fancy' fish

The only fish that reasonably come under the 'fancy' heading are salmon*, trout*, turbot and sole*, though if you are connected with an obsessive fisherman you may find yourself being obliged to find means of dealing with his catch of mullet, bream, mackerel and whiting.

Trout and sole are quickly cooked, so if they are obtainable practically kicking, they should only be thoroughly cleaned and frozen ready for use. The same goes for the fisherman's haul—hold it in readiness to fry in butter and make him eat it when it suits *you*.

Turbot steaks can be poached, drained and frozen very carefully each on a small foil plate, overwrapped in polythene.

63

The poaching liquor can be frozen separately for the eventual sauce, or made up and frozen in one operation if all the chosen sauce ingredients are good freezers.

If you are going to serve a salmon cold with salad, or made into a mousse, cook it first and freeze it in a rigid plastic container—*not* a metal mould. It is an unreasonable risk to freeze, cook and again chill even such a well-bred creature as a salmon.

Prawns and shrimps

Ready-frozen prawns and shrimps are not only absolutely free from hazard, but are cheaper bought in pound packets than tiny cartons—*and* they don't have to be peeled, which counts for a good deal in both time and money—but fresh ones are worth their while if you can obtain them in perfect condition and ideally boil them in your own pot.

A bag of peeled prawns in the freezer ensures a prawn cocktail or a *vol-au-vent* at half an hour's notice—the sauce and pastry cases for the *vol-au-vent* being already stocked in the freezer. Potted shrimps are another of the tedious items that repay being made in quantity, with a freezer life of up to five months. The advantage here is having more than the usual tiny, costly portions, and not having it taste of preservative.

Lobsters and crabs

Freshly caught and immediately cooked lobsters and crab should not be frozen for the sake of having them there, but with the intention of using them at a definite time. I don't know why it should be, but they are high on the list of delectables that one is inclined to leave in the freezer for 'another time' that doesn't always come as soon as it should.

This procrastination is less likely if the meat is made more readily accessible by being taken out of the shell and packed immediately in cartons for freezing. The two kinds of meat—flesh and coral in lobster, brown and white meat in crab—can be separated by a piece of foil inside the container.

Crustaceans frozen in the shell always take longer to thaw out than you think they will, and you are left to dig icy bits from the claws with a knitting needle. If you want to keep the shells for making a pretty dish, wash and dry them thoroughly and they will keep outside the freezer.

Mussels are above all shellfish in being something you can take or leave alone—and most people have very definite opinions either way.

Scampi

If you are devoted to them, it may be worth pointing out that the classic recipes for the over-rated and over-priced scampi—provençal, hongroise, à la crème,—can be made as well or better with mussels. This is as well as the luscious moules marinières or Italian mussel soup, or mussels with rice and cream sauce, or a mushroom and tomato sauce. Pardon me—my predilection is showing.

Mussels

In spite of all this poesy, you will be wise to exercise great caution in buying mussels from the fishmonger for freezing. He may have gone out in his waders at dawn and gathered them, but then again he may not. If you have absolute trust in your tradesman, buy at least a quart more of mussels than you think you will need—and *throw away* every last one of the molluscs that doesn't shut down like a trap at the merest approach to its open shell.

Mussels in the shells would obviously take up far too much freezer space. They must be cleaned in the usual exhaustive fashion, cooked in a little wine or water with a bay leaf until they open, and the resulting tender morsels packed in a waxed or plastic container with their delicate juices.

This would all be far too much like hard work for those who come out in spots at the very thought of a mussel. The other school of thought will consider it time well spent.

Classic meat dishes

Any of the classic meat dishes can be made to a favourite recipe and frozen, only having due regard for any proscribed ingredients, and being most scrupulous about quick cooling and skimming every trace of excess fat before freezing.

Your guide to freezing here will be the preparation time, particularly if you are making ready for any kind of celebration. One thinks of carbonnade of beef*, the meat cooked in ale, of ragoût* or *boeuf bourguignonne** with the sauce rich in red wine, of beef olives* with their minced meat filling, or even *boeuf en croûte* if you are really putting on the style and want to be quite sure that the puff pastry will not crumble or burn because you make it in haste.

This regal affair is best made and frozen uncooked. The pastry will keep the flavour and texture of the meat untouched. The meat should ideally be thawed before cooking.

Veal

One avoids the fearful risk of making veal even dryer than usual if its cooking has to be hurried, by preparing and freezing a blanquette* ready to have the cream and egg yolks added at reheating, or cooking escalopes* in stock and wine and adding cream during the leisured reheating. Pack veal or lamb dishes in their cooking liquor in plastic containers, or foil-lined casseroles, sealing very tightly. If bacon is included in the recipe cook and add it during reheating time if the dish is to be kept for more than four to six weeks.

Cooking meat with wine

When you use wine in freezer cooking, or when a recipe calls for meat to be flamed with brandy, it is usually a good

65

idea to reduce the amount of wine in the cooking and be prepared to add the rest and a little extra during reheating. Brandy should be poured on and allowed to flare at the very end of reheating. Alcohol is known to lose some of its potency during freezing, and is restored to the dish by these means.

If you cannot be sure at any given time just *how* you will want to serve some meat that is available for freezing, it can be cut into ample cubes and gently sautéed in oil before stewing in wine with minimum seasoning—white wine for pork, veal or lamb, red for beef or even venison if it should come your way and you have yet to find out how to cook it.

Freeze in lined dishes or in containers, labelling and dating each one very clearly indeed, because they will look alike when frozen. At the appropriate time, thaw the meat and use its own juices as a basis for the sauce. Pork treated in this fashion should not be kept for more than three months before final preparation. Other meat will be in good condition for up to six months.

Poultry dishes

When preparing rich poultry dishes for freezing, do any jointing of the bird before freezing—it will be quicker in thawing than if it were left whole—and use wine or spirits as you would with meat.

Chicken or duck can be cooked plainly and frozen for later embellishment as a cold dish. So can turkey if you ever have more than one in a year, but beware of goose. This fine old-fashioned favourite is far too greasy in all its forms to be a good freezer subject, and should be considered as a short-term prospect only.

Cassoulet

This rule can—*should*—be broken without a qualm for one good reason. The reason is cassoulet*, which none but the most dedicated ever serves. It takes a long time to prepare and longer to cook. For all that, it is a dish worth having a party *for*, containing as it does not only goose and/or duck but mutton, pork, brown breadcrumbs and haricot beans, as well as herbs and seasoning. It is Dickensian in its amplitude, and nobody ever forgets the eating of it.

Having broken pretty well all the freezer rules in one stroke, I must now say that cassoulet is a freezer subject by virtue of its immensity alone. No one person, or even two, can contemplate making and eating it in the same day. Though you can only make it by hours of cooking time, you can only freeze it for a limited time before the chosen occasion for serving it.

Ideally, if it is made and frozen at the beginning of the week, it should be eaten on Saturday. If you devote your week-end to its construction, organize the party for not later than Wednesday. The very maximum storage time should be two weeks. But try it, if only once, I beg.

It is almost bathos to talk about minor meat dishes now, but kebabs* should be considered for freezing ahead of serving. Not having to prepare them at speed means that you are that much less likely to split the tomatoes and drop them on your shoes, burst the onions, splinter the mushrooms and burn the shattered remains because you are called away just when they should be turned under the grill.

If you have a spit-roaster or oven with a kebab attachment, you will be spared the final indignity, at least.

Rabbits

People who enjoy rabbit, hare or pigeon, and particularly people who can shoot or snare their own supplies, are well served for specialities from the freezer. Rabbits are not as plump as they used to be, I do swear. If you have to cook two of them to make a meal for four people, you might just as well cook eight and only have to endure the one pang over their pathetic appearance.

The usual piece of pickled pork must be left out of the recipe you choose, but they do very well in the pot with stock instead of water, a bay leaf and a strip of finely-peeled lemon rind. Instead of forcemeat, cover the top of the meat during reheating with a mixture of breadcrumbs, herbs and butter and brown it crisply.

Rabbit flesh is really too dry to roast without a great deal of additional fat, so that must remain a cook-and-serve dish, not a cook-and-freeze.

I find hare* a gruesome subject to contemplate in detail, but fortunately everybody has her favourite method of preparation. Just as long as you avoid too much blood, you can't go wrong.

Pigeons

Pigeons are splendid freezer food, if only because they are like rabbits in being fiddlingly small. Also, they are plump at exactly the time of year when nobody really wants their dark meat, and skinny on scavengings in the winter, so the freezer redresses the balance.

Even the best-bred pigeons can be tough from so much exercise in their vain flight from the guns, and should be marinaded in an ordinary well-seasoned French dressing before cooking and freezing. Olive oil, fortunately, does not become rancid as quickly as animal fat or fish oil.

Game

This is convenient, because the older game birds that can often be bought at a most reasonable price late in the season require careful marinading before cooking, after which they

67

become one of the most useful winter meals that ever goes into a freezer.

All game* should be hung plucked and have any pellets extracted *before* freezing. If you attempt the hanging afterwards, the bird will promptly go so very bad that you will have to bury it in a remote place. Watch this point if you buy pheasants, partridge or grouse from a poulterer instead of shooting it or having it shot for you. He may well have had the birds in full feather in his own cold room, in which case you must get him to prepare them and put them straight into your own freezer.

Young game birds for roasting are really best frozen raw and cooked from the completely-thawed state, allowing more butter and bacon even than usual. If you really must roast them before freezing, seal them tightly in a container with their own juices, and be prepared to hand round additional sauce or gravy at the table.

Roux sauces

The more splendid sauces of the roux family are best considered as freezer prospects with a definite occasion in mind for them. Hollandaise and béarnaise, with their emulsion basis, will not be at all attractive when thawed as the emulsion separates, beyond all hope of whisking or beating it into shape again.

Béchamel sauce

Béchamel sauce, the basis of good onion, mushroom or cheese sauces, can be made in advance either in its entirety or to the point where the main ingredient can be mixed in for reheating and serving.

At one time the use of cornflour instead of flour in sauces enjoyed great popularity with authors of books on freezing. But if you have ever actually made and frozen a cornflour-based sauce you will wonder how the vogue ever caught on. The mass may not look curdled when it emerges from the freezer, but when reheated it will be extremely thick, gelatinous and utterly unappetizing. So when making flour-based sauces for the freezer stick to the usual recipe and forget the cornflour.

A lemon meringue pie filling is a total freezer failure for the same reason. It is thickened with cornflour and becomes gelatinous and wet after freezing and thawing.

Velouté sauces

The velouté sauces*—mustard, parsley or caper—are cooked with stock or a mixture of stock and milk instead of all milk, and these are even better subjects by temperament. Any necessary cream or egg yolk can be worked in during reheating. Do not be alarmed if the sauce comes out of the freezer with a pre-digested appearance. As the man said when he found the bad boy in the strawberry beds—beat it.

Brown sauces

The more hearty brown sauces* for serving with meat or poultry are based on the jellied stock that should always be in the freezer, and these present no problems. They can be made at any time, frozen in small containers, and will need no more than possibly a few spoonfuls of extra stock to thin them during reheating.

Curry sauce and dahl

Curry sauce* and dahl*—the cross between a soup and sauce made with lentils, curry paste, stock and onions—are worth making and freezing if you have the time and the taste. Freeze either or both in serving-size quantities in waxed or plastic containers—the dahl is thick enough for polythene bag freezing, only make sure that the bag is smooth and flat—and taste for seasoning on reheating.

With these two basics in stock, and a bag of rice already in the freezer, a curry meal can be produced in a quarter of an hour instead of two. Hard-boil some eggs, put them in the reheated curry sauce and place this inside a border of reheated rice. Or reheat already prepared meat cubes in curry sauce in a covered dish in the oven.

Tomato purée

Tomato purée* comes somewhere between sauce and vegetables proper. It has so many applications in cooking and is so tedious to make that it is small wonder that the Italians make such a good thing of exporting it. But even so, it is worth undertaking as an annual freezer commitment.

All you need is a vast box of tomatoes, a big pan and a nylon sieve. Tomato purée is never made successfully in a blender, unfortunately. The seeds disintegrate, and the texture is not as silky as it ought to be. Somewhere to sit down and a good programme on the radio are important adjuncts to the making of tomato purée—you will be pressing pulped tomatoes through the sieve for some considerable time, and will need to be distracted.

You will have to tell yourself that your purée will be envied by all who taste it, that it will stand as soup if diluted with stock, as tomato ketchup if some vinegar is worked in when you have forgotten to buy bottled sauce, will turn ravioli into something princely, and be a dream poured over braised pigeons. Every year, when I wear out the sieve yet again, I declare I will buy all future purée, but every year I am drawn back.

It is rather easier to make the rougher kind of tomato sauce* that goes as well with pasta but less well with other dishes. This has only to be reduced in the pan and keeps its

69

onions more or less intact. It helps in both cases if you don't bother to scald and skin the tomatoes before cooking, but just fish the loosened skins out of the pan at intervals during the cooking time.

A permanent supply of tomato purée covers all the pasta dishes that sit as easily on a party table as at a family meal. The fat tubes of cannelloni* can be stuffed with meat sauce and frozen in a tidy parcel—it doesn't matter that they will cleave together, because they will be cooked that way—reheated and placed in a shallow dish with purée and covered with grated parmesan on top.

Ravioli

If you have a delicatessen within reach that makes real ravioli—small cushions, not great bolsters—keep a supply in the freezer for simmering in stock and finishing with tomato purée and seasoning.

Ratatouille

Ratatouille*, the aromatic Provençal vegetable stew of tomatoes, onions, green peppers, courgettes, aubergines and herbs is a freezer essential, I think. It can stand cold and alone as a starter to any meal, be served hot or cold with chops, cold meat or raised pies, as a side dish when salad is unreasonably dear or weather stricken, or as an extra vegetable for the hungry or unexpected. Apart from these talents, it *looks* so special.

Meat pies

Home-made raised pies are so infinitely preferable to shop-bought, and so satisfying to make, that they can well be considered for freezing. They are better on picnics than sandwiches and can be served grandly garnished or just plain, depending on the occasion.

For freezing, several small pies are preferable to one large one, with a chance of leftover pieces being wasted. Thawing time is shorter and the result more satisfactory than if a solid mass of meat has to thaw over a long period.

Make raised pies of pork or game—not veal and ham unless the freezer time is going to be very short—with hot-water crust according to any recipe.

Only omit the traditional hard-boiled eggs, and do not follow the rule of filling the pie with jellied stock immediately after cooking. Make and freeze the stock from the meat bones and trimmings, seasoning it very well indeed, and keep it in a separate container. Warm it just to pouring point when the pie is half-thawed. Only then pour the stock into the pie through the funnel in the middle, and the still-cold meat will set it quickly before it can damp and spoil the inside of the crisp crust.

Ordinary pastry comes under the plain cookery heading,

◀ Freeze Victoria Sandwich layers separately. Sandwich and decorate later with cream and fruit from the freezer

1
Assorted biscuits can either be baked and frozen, or made from frozen biscuit mixture

2
Chocolate Dairy Cream Sponge decorated with a mixture of concentrated orange juice, frozen egg white and sugar, whisked together for a fluffy topping

3
Baked choux buns freeze well and can be filled with whipping cream from the freezer. Coat them with freshly made chocolate icing

4
Assorted small cakes can be made by cutting shapes from frozen slabs of baked Victoria sandwich mixture, and decorated with butter icing from the freezer

1

2

3

4

but there are refinements that only become practicable for the rushed or heavy-handed by using a freezer. French flan pastry heads this field—it may offer a childlike pleasure in breaking eggs on to a board instead of into a bowl, and the working of eggs, flour, sugar and butter with the fingers is a recurring fascination. But the rolling! I prefer to forget the times I have followed a piece of French flan round and round the kitchen, thwarting its efforts to bind itself round the rolling pin like a boa-constrictor or to fasten me on to the far wall.

Flan pastry

Flan pastry can also be frozen uncooked in small tartlet tins, ready for filling with strawberries, redcurrants or apricot-halves with their strained, thickened juice about them. These serve equally well as puddings or party pieces.

To be frank, I think you have to be a particularly avid cook, or one of those fortunates who can cook with one hand and exercise the dog with the other, before you can contemplate puff pastry without a quiver.

If you can make it well anyway, it will be even better after a frozen spell. If you are really not very good at it, a freezer will improve on your efforts. If you are plain ordinary bad at it, never achieving more than a yellowish, miserable-looking laminate, don't bother any more. Buy it in packets, and be grateful.

Frozen *vol-au-vent** and bouchée cases, ready to cook, are everybody's friend. I only wish they were produced in eight-inch sizes, but to date they are not. Relieved of the anxiety of propping up pastry cases which go lopsided in the oven, one can use the time and energy saved to prepare several kinds of fillings.

Choux pastry

Choux pastry* for cream buns, éclairs or profiteroles, or savoury gougères*, if your will or ability is going to carry you that far, is another freezer-dominated commodity.

Cream buns made in a hurry or as a single item are likely to fail from lack of beating, and waste fuel because the high cooking temperature is wasteful to reach for a small amount of cooking.

The choux is made and cooked in the ordinary way, each cooked piece being split to let out the steam and cooled on a wire tray before being packed in a box or tin for freezing. The cases can either be frozen in a polythene box or they can be filled with whipped whipping cream and coated with melted chocolate and then frozen. Filled éclairs* will need about an hour to thaw. Gougères cases can also be frozen ready to be filled later with a cheese or meat mixture.

All these efforts are worth making. Small choux buns can be contrived into grand puddings by several methods of filling, icing and saucing, and it is all too much trouble to make *at the same time* as the rest of a meal.

Meringues

The same can be said of meringues*, with their long, slow oven-drying and their swift deterioration into sugary sadness. Admittedly they keep well in a truly air-tight container, but they store even better in a freezer. Small meringues for sandwiching with cream, even smaller ones for decorating cakes or puddings, or the mixture smoothed into eight-inch circles on non-stick paper for filling with strawberries and cream, or meringues made with ground almonds or hazelnuts for a galette, can be made at any time and frozen in boxes ready for filling.

Once frozen, they are slightly less delicate than usual, but label the box 'With Care' for safety.

If you do have a calamity and break meringues in the freezer, crush the pieces to finest crumbs with a rolling pin or in a blender, and put them back in the freezer in a bag. Use them instead of castor sugar on top of jam sponge cakes, or stir them into whipped cream for serving with fruit or pudding. A home freezer never lets even its mistake be wasted.

Nearly all the splendid—i.e. time-consuming—puddings can be made at leisure and stored in a home freezer. When you know that the sure way to make a soufflé fall into a swoon is to indicate that you want it to hurry, it becomes only reasonable to make it for the freezer when *you* are not in a hurry. A hot soufflé cannot be baked and frozen, which is rather a pity, but you can always pretend you don't like those anyway, and make a cold one.

For freezer pudding purposes, it is worth finding your nearest supplier of whipping cream, which, when whipped, freezes more satisfactorily than rich double cream.

Soufflés or mousses

Make soufflés* or mousses* according to your usual recipe, and freeze as soon as the mixture is set. A soufflé will have to be frozen in a waxed paper case, with the additional protection of a plastic box or biscuit tin, but the firmer mousse can be unmoulded and set on the *lid* of a plastic box or bowl, the container itself put over the top and sealed down. Just be careful to mark the *bottom* of the container 'This Way Up', or you may find yourself with something to regret.

The upside-down trick works equally well with a large meringue, an airy sponge cake, or an ambitious bombe of ice-cream. By taking the bottom off the top, so to speak, you are saved the nerve-wracking procedure of trying to fish the cake out without digging your finger-tips into its vitals. In fact, you can avoid touching the thing at all by putting two crossed strips of doubled foil on the lid below the confection, and using the overlapping ends as convenient handles for transport.

Ice-cream

It is always worth making ice-cream for the freezer. Ailing children will always eat it, whatever else they scorn, and be nourished in spite of themselves. Healthy adults will simply be astonished and well-pleased. The comparatively rapid effect of the freezer does away with the tedium of beating the half-frozen mixture and all the waiting about that it involves.

Use an up-to-date recipe—the old-fashioned ones are full of warnings and isinglass—and use double cream in this one case. After that, ice-cream is no more trouble to prepare than the humblest custard.

Suédoise

When you want to go one better than a fruit fool—and who wouldn't—you can make and freeze a *suédoise*. Fresh or frozen raspberries, apricots or plums are puréed, sweetened and set with gelatine for freezing in an ordinary jelly mould.

A *suédoise* has a finer texture than a fruit fool, and more *joie de vivre* than a mousse. The advantage gained by freezing the mixture comes in the serving—at room temperature, particularly in summer weather, it is very inclined to start collapsing. Served straight from the fridge, it is usually too cold to be full-flavoured. Taken out of the freezer and left in a coolish place for about two hours before serving with its bowl of whipped cream, and only unmoulded before the dash to the dining-room, it is exactly right.

Hot puddings seem to have gone right out of fashion as far as festive meals are concerned—probably because the single-handed, freezerless cook, poor thing, depends on the ritual of cold-hot-cold for her menus. By contrast, the only thing the home-freezing cook has to beware of is the chance of becoming over-zealous and putting out more food to reheat than she has room for in or on the stove. This happens, I promise you, so count your burners first.

Pancakes

Of the likely hot puddings, pancakes* is *the* one that cannot be served without a great deal of flushed to-and-froing between courses.

So make a comfortable pile of pancakes when you feel so inclined, and freeze them stacked with foil or non-stick baking paper between them. They will regain their bendable quality within a few minutes of coming out of the freezer and being separated. They can be filled with jam or stewed fruit flavoured with liqueur, an appropriate sauce of strained jam fruit juice poured round them in a flat dish, and left to reheat under a loose foil covering in a cool oven while the main course is eaten.

There is no point yet known to science, and certainly not one acknowledged by any home-freezing addict, where the freezing of difficult, delicious and delicate food really has to stop. I have been trying to get this message home to my plain-cooking, plain cousin for years, but I think she is beyond redemption.

You, I know, are quite different. *You* will work your way through *The Birds Eye Book of Home Freezing,* and in finding what has been left out that you would have put in, you will be making your own way towards your own ultimate capacity for freezer cooking. And you'll like it that way!

Some Seasonal Suggestions

Here are some ideas for getting the best out of your freezer. Since no two people or households share the same tastes—or the same freezer!—a comprehensive seasonal list is impossible. The best recipe is 'two parts commonsense and one part inspiration'. And never be afraid to add a dash of trial by error. Your friends and family need never know!

Spring

March

As the weather gets warmer, prepare to plant a selection of herbs, e.g. parsley, chives, marjoram, borage and balm. These can all be grown successfully from seed. Roots of thyme and mint are also useful.

Think ahead and plan for children's Easter holiday. Good stocks of beefburgers, fish fingers and pies will be useful.

Easter week-end can be planned in advance. On Easter Sunday, serve melon and pineapple from the freezer as a starter. The turkey or a large chicken with the usual trimmings will make a good family main course along with a selection of vegetables. Prepare and freeze a chocolate soufflé for sweet. For those living near the coast, whitebait should be available. Lamb should be getting cheaper at this time—purchase while still frozen.

April

Take a breather before preparing for a busy season ahead! Ideal time to prepare for dinner parties. For example:

Menu 1

Pâté   —prepare, cook and freeze without coating of butter or bacon. Cover with melted butter when thawing.

| Chicken Marengo | —cook and freeze. Freeze croûtons of fried bread for garnish. Freeze rice to accompany. |
| Profiteroles | —make choux cases and freeze. Fill when thawed. |

Menu 2

Prawn Cocktail	—order/purchase prawns.
Boeuf Stroganoff	—cook and freeze omitting sour cream. Stir in when reheating.
Raspberry Pavlova	—Bake and freeze meringue case. Fill before serving.

May

Salmon should be available and sea trout are in season. Buy fresh for freezing.

Garden rhubarb should be ready for cutting. Young stalks can be cut up and frozen dry or in syrup and can be used for pies, crumbles and fools later in the year.

Time to plan for a summer barbecue. Assemble kebabs on stainless steel or wooden skewers before freezing. Order supplies of corn-on-the-cob, beefburgers and chicken. If there is room in the freezer, buy a good stock of baps and French bread for the occasion.

Picnic preparations can be carried out. Sausage rolls and meat pasties can be made. Sandwiches, sliced loaves and bread rolls will also be useful.

Summer

June

Asparagus should be ready for picking, blanching and freezing. Early garden peas should also be ready.

Gooseberries will be ripe and ready for freezing. They should be topped and tailed and can be packed dry for future use in such items as pies and tarts or used for jam making.

Imported apricots should be coming into the shops and these can be frozen dry or in syrup.

July

Raspberries will be ready for picking and freezing. Jam can be made later from fruit which has been packed dry. White, red and black currants become plentiful and these must be topped and tailed before packing dry or in syrup. Ideal for jam and jelly making later in the year. Peaches should be ripening and ready for freezing.

French beans should be at their best and ready for blanching and freezing. Those who grow artichokes should freeze them in July and August.

Crabs and lobsters are at their cheapest at this time but they must be very fresh.

Remember *not* to turn the electricity supply off when going on holiday.

August

Melons and pineapple will be cheap and plentiful and can be frozen together in syrup for a refreshing fruit cocktail. These fruits can also be frozen with others for fruit salads.

Broad beans will be at their best and tomatoes will be ready for picking. Cheaper, softer tomatoes in the shops can be puréed and packaged for use in many dishes.

The salmon season finishes this month so there will be no more fresh salmon available.

For those living in country areas, venison will be at its best.

Autumn

September

Herbs should be harvested for freezing. They need not be chopped but can be crumbled when frozen. Apples and pears will be ready for freezing and damsons and plums will be ripe. A glut of the latter can be frozen for future use in jam making. Blackberries will be plentiful in the country. Cook them gently and mix with stewed apple before freezing for future use in pies and turnovers.

October

Green peppers, courgettes and aubergines should be at favourable prices. These can be frozen separately or mixed together and cooked in a ratatouille before freezing.

Any cauliflowers remaining in the garden can be prepared and frozen.

This is the best season for Scotch beef and prices should begin to fall.

November

Root vegetables will be at their cheapest and useful 'stew-packs' can be assembled and frozen using carrots, onions, parsnips and swede. These can be used in soups and stews later.

Warming winter meals can be prepared in advance. Meat pies and puddings, cottage pies and assorted casseroles can be cooked, packed and frozen for winter days.

Children's Christmas holidays lie ahead and stocks of

sausages, fish fingers, fish cakes and beefburgers will be required for high teas and suppers. Individual meals could be frozen in preparation for Christmas shopping days when there is little time for cooking.

Christmas day preparations can begin—to relieve the pressure later—and mince pies should be prepared and frozen uncooked in foil patty tins. Breadcrumbs and sausage meat for stuffings and accompaniments can be prepared and packed.

If there is room, a frozen turkey can be bought in advance and stored in the freezer.

Winter

December
Final Christmas preparations can be made early in December. Extra commercially-frozen vegetables should be ordered and bacon rolls can be made and frozen. Bread sauce will freeze successfully and brandy butter for the Christmas pudding could be prepared and frozen.

The remains of the turkey can be cut up and frozen in sauce for a fricassée. Stock made from the bones will be useful if kept in the freezer and used for soups and casseroles.

January
Winter broccoli should be ready for picking, preparation and freezing. Brussels sprouts should also be at their best in December and January.

Look out for cheap Seville oranges which can be frozen and used for marmalade later in the year.

Those living on the coast should look out for cod, halibut and skate. Scallops will also be in season.

Game will have been plentiful for a while and prices will be lower. Prepare as for immediate use, but do not stuff. Partridge and pheasant freeze well.

February
This is an ideal time to defrost and clean out the freezer, while stocks are low after the Christmas season.

Look out for cheap frozen turkeys which can be stored and used at Easter.

Good time to prepare for a future children's party. Order éclairs, sausages, sausage rolls, as well as ice-cream and mousse, from a bulk supplier.

Make sandwiches and small cakes and prepare rounds of cooked Victoria sandwich mixture for the birthday cake.

Vegetable Blanching Chart

VEGETABLE	PREPARATION	BLANCHING TIME (MINS)
ASPARAGUS	Wash in ice cold water. Cut into lengths to fit container. Do not tie into bunches. Blanch. Pack tips to stalks.	3–5
BEANS, BROAD	Shell, sort by size, blanch and pack.	3
BEANS FRENCH OR RUNNER	Select young, tender beans. Wash thoroughly. **French** Trim ends and blanch. **Runner** Slice thickly and blanch.	3 2
BROCCOLI	Select compact heads with tender stalks. Trim stalks evenly. Wash thoroughly. Drain well. Blanch. Pack tips to stalks.	3
BRUSSELS SPROUTS	Select firm, tight, small, evenly sized sprouts. Remove outer leaves. Wash thoroughly. Blanch.	4–6
CARROTS	Select young carrots with good colour. Scrub, cut off tops, trim ends, wash well. Blanch. Freeze whole.	5
CAULIFLOWER	Separate heads into sprigs. Wash thoroughly. Blanch.	3
CORN ON THE COB	Select young, yellow kernels. Remove husk and silks. Blanch.	6–10
HERBS	Chop or freeze in the sprig.	–

Vegetable Blanching Chart

VEGETABLE	PREPARATION	BLANCHING TIME (MINS)
LEEKS	Wash and slice. Blanch.	1
MUSHROOMS	Sauté in margarine, or blanch in deep oil	1
ONIONS FRIED, WHOLE	Slice, flour and blanch in oil. Trim small button onions before blanching.	3
PEAS	Selected young peas, shell and sort by size. Blanch.	1½
POTATOES	Cooked roast, duchesse or croquettes should be prepared in normal way.	–
CHIPS	Peel and 'chip' in the usual way. Water blanch. Then oil blanch.	2 1
ROOT VEGETABLES (eg. TURNIP, SWEDE)	Dice and blanch. Can also be frozen after full cooking and mashing with butter.	3
SPINACH	Select young leaves and trim. Wash well in running water. Drain. Blanch.	1½–2
TOMATOES	Slice and pack alone or as purée.	–

Fruit Chart

FRUIT		PREPARATION
APPLES 	**Sliced**	Peel, core and slice. Steam blanch for 2 minutes. Cool in iced water.
	Purée	Peel, core, and stew in minimum water, sweetened or unsweetened. Sieve and cool.
APRICOTS		Freeze whole, or sliced with stones removed. Best frozen in syrup.
CHERRIES		Remove stalks, stone, wash and dry. Best frozen in syrup.
GOOSEBERRIES 	**Whole**	Top and tail — wash and dry. Freeze dry, in sugar or syrup.
GRAPEFRUIT 		Leave whole or segment before freezing. Can be sweetened.
GRAPES 		Remove stalks, halve, remove pips and freeze in syrup.
GREENGAGES 	**Sweet**	Pack dry or in sugar — 4 oz per lb.
	Cooking	Syrup — $\frac{1}{2}$ lb sugar to 1 pint water.
LEMONS 		Leave whole or segment before freezing. Freeze peel for grating.
MELONS		Dice or cut into balls. Freeze in syrup.
ORANGES 		Leave whole or segment before freezing. Freeze peel for grating.

Fruit Chart

FRUIT	PREPARATION
PEACHES	Remove skin. Remove stones and slice. Freeze in syrup.
PEARS	**Cooking** Peel, core and cook. Freeze in syrup. **Eating** Peel, core and cook for $1\frac{1}{2}$ minutes. Freeze in syrup.
PINEAPPLES	Dice before freezing. Can be sweetened first.
PLUMS	Wipe skins, halve and discard stones. Freeze in syrup.
RHUBARB	Cook and freeze in syrup.
SOFT FRUIT **STRAWBERRIES**	Choose firm, clean dry fruit. Remove stalks. Freeze dry.
RASPBERRIES	Choose firm, clean dry fruit. Remove stalks. Freeze dry.
LOGANBERRIES	Choose firm, clean dry fruit. Remove stalks. Freeze dry.
BLACKBERRIES	Choose firm, clean dry fruit. Remove stalks. Freeze dry.
CURRANTS	**Whole** Wash, dry, top and tail. Freeze dry. **Purée** Wash, top and tail. Cook to a purée with brown sugar but little or no water.

Freezer Facts, Figures and Recipes
(An alphabetical reference list)

Ambient temperature

A term referring to the temperature of the air *outside* the freezer. The thermostat on a freezer operates according to the temperature inside the freezer. In a high ambient temperature the motor will cut in and out more often than in a low ambient.

Apple crumble

Preparation. The dish may be prepared from frozen slices of apple and a frozen rubbed-in mixture of fat, flour and sugar in the proportions 1½ : 4 : 2, baked and served. Alternatively it can be assembled from unfrozen ingredients and then frozen before cooking.

Place ¾ lb. of prepared apple slices in each deep foil pie dish and sprinkle with 2 oz. demerara sugar. Spread 8 oz. crumble over each and press down gently. Freeze raw or cook at 375°F. (Gas Mark 5) for about 45 minutes.

Freezing. Overwrap each apple crumble in a polythene bag, seal and label.

Freezer Life. Up to 6 months.

To Use. Remove from polythene bag and reheat a cooked crumble straight from the freezer at 350°F. (Gas Mark 4) for about 30 minutes. Cover with foil if the top becomes very brown.

Place frozen uncooked crumble in the oven at 350°F. (Gas Mark 4) for 30 minutes then raise heat to 425°F. (Gas Mark 7) for a further 20 minutes to brown the top.

Apples

Firm eating apples can be wiped, sliced thinly and steam blanched for 2 minutes. They can then be frozen without sugar for later use in French flans. Cooking apples are peeled, cored, the bruised parts removed and cooked in a very little water until they can be beaten to a purée with a blender or wooden spoon and then sieved. A quantity of apples can be cooked with vanilla sugar and a twist of lemon rind for use as pie filling or for serving with custard. Use about 2 teaspoons of vanilla sugar and 2 teaspoons of castor sugar to each pint of purée. Apple sauce for serving with pork or duck can be frozen with one or two fresh leaves of sage in each pint container. Cool the apple purée before freezing.

Freezing. Pack apple slices in a lidded polythene box, with double foil between layers. Purée can be frozen in rigid wax or polythene containers or in polythene bags with HEAD-SPACE, sealed and labelled as to flavouring.

Freezer Life. Up to one year.

To Use. Dry frozen apple slices can be arranged in a flan case as soon as they have thawed enough to be separated without damage. Purée used as filling for covered pies is thawed at room temperature until it can be spread out in the pie dish. Heat sweet and savoury sauces in a covered container in the oven or over gentle heat in a saucepan. Avoid overheating as this will produce a dry sauce and warmed-up flavour.

Apricots

Preparation. Taste apricots in the shop before buying a quantity for freezing. If they seem fibrous, or hard though described as 'ripe', do not buy. Wipe the skin of the fruit, but do not peel. Cut into halves and take out the stone. Only attempt to prepare a small quantity at a time, to avoid discoloration of the cut flesh. Small, well-flavoured and perfectly ripe apricots can be frozen whole.

Freezing. Put the halved apricots quickly into plastic or waxed containers, half-filled with 30% sugar SYRUP. Leave HEADSPACE. Label the containers.

Freezer Life. Fruit frozen without stones will keep for up to a year, with stones for about 6 months.

To Use. Thaw in containers at room temperature for 4 or 5 hours, or in the refrigerator overnight.

Artichokes

Preparation. Globe artichokes cannot be frozen whole, but the 'fonds' freeze well. Choose large artichokes, the outer leaves not too widely-spread. Holding them firmly on a board, cut through the tops with a sharp knife, about an inch from the tip. Pull off two or three layers of the lower outer leaves. Put the reduced artichokes in a large pan of boiling salted water, without overcrowding. Cook for 15–20 minutes, according to size. Cool them quickly under running cold water. Pull off remaining leaves and discard, cut out the 'choke' with the edge of a spoon. Clear remaining leaves from around the 'fonds'.

Freezing. Put the 'fonds' side by side in a plastic box, filling the box with layers separated by double pieces of foil. Seal and label.

Freezer Life. Up to 6 months.

To Use. For serving cold with vinaigrette dressing, leave the 'fonds' at room temperature for about 1 hour.

Aubergines

Preparation. Choose firm, ripe aubergines of a uniform size, with a rich gloss on the skins. Do not choose for freezing any which look at all wrinkled or dull. Do not peel, but cut small specimens lengthways and larger ones into half-inch slices. BLANCH by steaming for 5 minutes. Cool rapidly and dry with a clean cloth.

Freezing. Interleave slices with double greaseproof paper or aluminium foil. Pack in polythene box or waxed container. Seal and label.

Freezer Life. About 6 months.

To Use. Use the aubergines direct from the freezer as an ingredient in prepared dishes. For use as an extra vegetable, half-thaw by leaving at room temperature for an hour or so, drain off any liquid and fry in butter or oil until completely hot and lightly browned.

Autolysis

A sort of self-digestion process which occurs in meat and fish after slaughter or killing. Carcasses are deliberately hung or aged for a definite period of time so that enzymes in the flesh can effect autolysis to produce a good flavour and texture in the meat.

In fish, however, autolysis proceeds at a much more rapid rate so that it very soon goes beyond a desirable degree and produces undesirable flavours.

If meats were hung for too long they also would become 'sour' but the process is arrested by cooking or quick freezing the raw meat. This is one reason why fish is more perishable than most meat and why it should not be frozen unless very, very fresh.

Bacon

Bacon is cured by a method similar to ham curing. Sometimes raw bacon fat becomes pink when frozen but if the bacon is cooked thoroughly this is masked and the bacon has a normal appearance. If a cooked dish requires snippets or rolls of bacon these can be included before freezing but the freezer life of the dish may be reduced as the salt used in curing hastens the development of rancidity. Alternatively, if longer storage of the dish is desired, cooked bacon may be added to the dish during reheating. Both smoked and un-smoked bacon rashers may be interleaved with plastic sheeting, overwrapped in foil and kept frozen for 6 weeks.

Bacteria

Microscopic organisms found everywhere, on the skin, on work surfaces, in the soil, the air and on meat, fish, fruit and vegetables. Some are useful and their growth actively encouraged as in the production of yoghurt and the development of flavour during hanging of game. Other types of bacteria may bring about changes in food which make it unpleasant to eat and a few types can cause illness.

Freezing and storage of food in a home freezer at or below −18°C. (0°F.) halts bacteriological activity completely. Normal bacteriological growth is gradually resumed after thawing as the bacteria recover from the shock of freezing. So thawed food should be treated as though it has never been frozen. It should not be repeatedly thawed and refrozen as this has an undesirable effect on texture and flavour. If it has been cooked after thawing refreezing is perfectly acceptable.

Bananas

Do not include slices of banana in any fruit salad or pudding for the freezer. The thawed product will be brown and slimy.

Baskets

Chest-type freezers are fitted with plastic-covered wire baskets which fit on to the ledge beneath the lid. They are fitted as standard in large freezers, bought separately in small models. They are an aid to convenience in finding stored food by dividing the close-packed contents of the freezer, but are not absolutely essential. Some upright freezers are fitted with removable baskets as well as or instead of shelves.

Batter

Preparation. Make Yorkshire pudding or pancake batter in the usual way, using 5 oz. flour and 1 egg to ½ pint milk. Leave to stand for 1 hour.

Freezing. Pour the prepared batter in ½ pint or 1 pint quantities into plastic or waxed containers leaving HEAD-SPACE. Seal the containers and stand them upright in the freezer until the batter is frozen or pour batter into lightly greased patty tins, freeze and overwrap with polythene.

Freezer Life. 6–8 months.

To Use. Leave the batter to thaw at room temperature in its opened container for at least 2 hours depending on quantity. Use for coating fish for frying, or for fritters, or for PANCAKES or YORKSHIRE PUDDING. Cook individual puddings direct from the freezer.

Béarnaise sauce

Unsuitable for freezing. See HOLLANDAISE SAUCE.

Béchamel sauce

See WHITE SAUCE.

Beef

Most cuts of beef, except the fatty BRISKET, will freeze well, raw or cooked. Leftovers of beef are better frozen in cubes for later cooking than in slices for serving cold, when the meat may become dry. See also MEAT, PURCHASE OF, FREEZ-ING, PACKING. Also STEAKS, BOEUF BOURGUIGNONNE, CASSEROLES, CARBONNADE OF BEEF, RAGOUT, BEEF OLIVES.

Freezer Life. For lean raw beef. Up to 9 months

Beef olives

Preparation. Beef olives made for freezing should be prepared with meat not previously frozen. Slices of chuck steak or skirt are beaten thin and flat, rolled round a filling. The following proportions will fill half a dozen ¼ lb. slices of meat—½ lb. minced veal, an onion, 2 tablespoons of fresh or frozen white breadcrumbs, 2 teaspoons of fresh or frozen mixed herbs, an egg, salt and pepper. Chop the onion finely, soften in butter without browning, mix with the minced veal, breadcrumbs, herbs and seasoning. Moisten with the egg. Spread over the centre of the meat slices, roll up and tie with thread. Brown the rolled meat quickly in olive oil in a stewpan. Remove from the pan to a plate, and brown two sliced onions, a carrot and a stick of celery in the oil. Pour on ½ pint of STOCK, add a fresh or frozen BOUQUET GARNI. Bring to the boil, lower the heat and replace the meat olives. Cook in a slow oven 325°F. (Gas Mark 3) for 1–1½ hours until the meat is tender. Cool by standing the closely-lidded pan in the sink under running cold water.

Freezing. Strain the sauce. Put the cooled meat, immersed in its own sauce, in a foil baking dish or foil-lined oven dish. Cover with an extra piece of foil. Freeze solid, remove from the dish, overwrap, seal and label.

Freezer Life. 3 or 4 months.

To Use. Stand foil-covered package at room temperature for about ½ hour then remove foil carefully. Place beef olives and sauce in a thick saucepan and heat gently until olives are

83

hot throughout. If sauce is thin, thicken with a little flour. Before serving, remove thread from beef olives.

Beetroot

Preparation. Consider the availability of freezer space before deciding to freeze beetroot. Choose very small, preferably garden-grown beets, wash, trim and cook slowly in a little vinegar and water in a covered dish in the oven rather than boiling them quickly in a pan. Cool, skin and cut into thin strips rather than cubes or slices. Golf-ball size beets can be skinned and left whole for freezing.

Freezing. Pack into waxed containers or polythene bags.

Freezer Life. Up to 6 months.

To Use. Leave the beetroots in their opened containers at room temperature for 2 or 3 hours.

Belly pork

This cut of meat is not good freezer material, being largely composed of fat which quickly becomes rancid. Rancid meat is not bad in the sense of being poisonous, but its flavour and odour are objectionable.

Biscuit mixes

Preparation. Biscuit mixes rich in butter and sugar are usually a nuisance to roll and cut when freshly made. The nuisance is abated by making two or three times the usual quantity of mixture and freezing the surplus in weighed-out quantities to provide the number of biscuits that would usually be made in one session.

Freezing. Shape small quantities of the biscuit mix into brick shapes, parcel in foil and overwrap in a polythene bag. Alternatively, pre-freeze the mixture for about 15 minutes, unwrapped, roll and cut into shapes. Freeze the shapes in a plastic box, with foil between the layers to prevent them sticking together. Label package.

Freezer Life. Up to 6 months.

To Use. Thaw the parcelled mix until it is of a rolling con-sistency, then roll and shape. Leave prepared biscuits at room temperature until thawed. Cook both mixtures in the usual way.

Blackberries

Preparation. Choose only firm, dry, ripe fruit for freezing. Check for and discard any with signs of worm or mould. Do not wash the fruit before freezing. To every prepared pound of blackberries, add the stripped berries from two or three large sprays of elderberry if liked.

Freezing. Put the blackberries and elderberries in poly-thene bags, tie loosely and freeze as for RASPBERRIES.

Freezer Life. Up to 1 year.

To Use. Put the frozen blackberries into a pan with a lot of sugar and possibly two or three leaves of frozen balm, but no water. When thawing begins, stir from time to time to prevent scorching before the juice runs freely. Partly thaw the fruit before using as a pie filling.

Blackcurrants

Preparation. Choose ripe, shiny blackcurrants for freezing, avoiding little wizened ones. Top and tail the berries, discarding any with broken skins or traces of mould. Wash the fruit by putting it in a colander or wire basket and swishing under the cold water tap. Drain carefully in colander. Blackcurrants intended for pie-filling can be cooked almost to a pulp, without any additional water, but with brown sugar.

Freezing. Uncooked fruit is put in 1 or 1½ lb. quantities in large polythene bags, the bags loosely tied and laid flat on wire cake-cooling trays inside the freezer until the fruit is firm. Shake the fruit down inside the bag, without making too bulky a package, expel as much air as possible by pressing gently over the surface of the bag from the bottom upwards. Tie the necks of the bags firmly with plastic-covered wire ties, and stack the bags one on the other for storage. Cooked puréed blackcurrants should be packed in plastic bowls or boxes with tightly fitting lids, or in WAXED CONTAINERS with HEADSPACE.

Freezer Life. Up to 1 year.

To Use. Leave the blackcurrants in their bags in the refrigerator overnight, turning them out on to a dish and leaving at room temperature for 2 or 3 hours if they are to be served cold with cream. If they are to be cooked after freezing, turn them directly into a pan or oven-dish, sugar freely, and cook gently to the required stage. Frozen cooked and puréed fruit, for use in pies or as a pudding, can be turned out of the container after being held under running hot water for a moment and fully thawed in a bowl over a pan of hot water or left at room temperature overnight.

Blanching

A term used to describe the short, rapid heating (usually in boiling water) of fresh vegetables before freezing. Blanching is necessary to halt the activity of enzymes within the substance of the vegetables. If left unchecked, enzyme activity would bring about gradual deterioration of eating quality during storage. The colour, flavour and texture of the food would ultimately be so changed as to render it unpalatable.

For best results, vegetables should be blanched in a pan

large enough to hold at least eight pints of fast boiling water, without boiling over. Prepare the vegetables as indicated in individual entries, and put in *no more than* 1 lb. quantities in a blanching basket, salad drainer or colander which will fit inside the pan when the lid is closed. Immerse the blanching container in the boiling water, cover the pan, and take the blanching time from the moment the water comes back to the boil. See individual entries for timing. It is important to time the blanching exactly—too short a time will not adequately destroy the enzyme activity, too long may result in mushy or broken vegetables on final cooking. As soon as blanching is completed, take the vegetables in their container from the pan and immediately immerse in a large bowl of iced water. Cooling time will be about double the blanching time. Drain the cooled vegetables thoroughly. Pack and freeze immediately, according to instructions in individual entries.

Blanquette of veal   *Preparation*. For 4 portions trim and cut 1½ lb. of veal into equal sized chunks and cook gently for ½ hour in water to cover with a fresh or frozen bouquet garni, salt and a few peppercorns. Remove scum and add 8 peeled but unsliced shallots and 3 carrots cut into quarters. Continue to boil for about 40 minutes until the meat is tender. Remove shallots and cool these. Discard carrots. Strain cooking liquor and reserve. Make a creamy white sauce by the roux method using 2 oz. butter, 2 oz. flour and cooking liquor made up to 1 pint with water. Season with salt and pepper. Cool. Sauté 4 oz. button mushrooms, drain and add to the blanquette.

Freezing. Place meat and shallots in a foil-lined 2½ pint casserole and immerse in sauce. Cover with casserole lid and freeze. When frozen wrap tightly with foil and pack in a polythene bag. Seal and label.

Freezer Life. 4–6 months.

To Use. Remove from packaging and heat in double boiler. Beat 1 egg with ¼ pint single cream and blend mixture into sauce. Adjust seasoning before serving.

Boeuf bourguignonne   The classic recipes usually call for streaky bacon. Its addition before freezing reduces the freezer life of the dish and it can be cooked and added during reheating if desired. Carrot should be added to the bourguignonne half-way through cooking to prevent it becoming soft and mushy.

Preparation. Cook for the freezer in multiples of the basic 4-portion recipe. You will need 1½ lb. chuck steak cut into large cubes, oil for frying, 1 carrot, leek and onion, a bouquet

◀ Frozen bread dough, tomato sauce, herbs and grated cheese combined to make a pizza which is decorated with anchovies and olives before baking

1
Short pastry, apple purée and apple slices from the freezer quickly assembled to make an impressive French Apple Flan

2
Frozen pastry *vol-au-vent* shapes baked and filled with white sauce and prawns from the freezer – an ideal buffet or supper dish

3
Frozen bread dough provides versatility for the enthusiastic cook who can produce plain and fancy breads in no time at all

4
Commercially baked bread, wrapped, labelled and ready for freezing

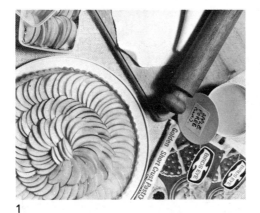

1

2

3

4

garni, 1 pint beef stock, ¼ bottle red wine, 1 oz. flour, 12 button onions, 6 button mushrooms, 2 oz. chopped fried bacon.

Heat the oil in a large casserole and brown the meat quickly on all sides. Remove from casserole and sprinkle with a little salt and ground black pepper. Chop the carrot, leek and onion and brown in the oil. Remove the carrot and replace meat. Add a fresh or frozen bouquet garni, beef stock and red wine. Cook, covered, in the oven at 290°F. (Gas Mark 2) for 1 hour. Stir in the flour, replace the carrot and cook for a further hour. Peel 12 small onions and cook these gently in oil. Add the mushrooms and fry these for 1–2 minutes. Add the onions and mushrooms to the casserole. Fried bacon may be added now or later when the bourguignonne is reheated to be eaten. Cool by standing the tightly-lidded casserole under running cold water.

To Freeze. Place the cooled bourguignonne in one or more foil-lined ovenproof dishes, cover all meat with sauce and freeze. When solid, cover the surface with more foil, wrap tightly and overwrap in a polythene bag. Seal and label.

Freezer Life. 3–4 months without bacon. Up to 6 weeks with bacon.

To Use. Place opened foil package in its ovenproof dish, cover and heat in the oven at 350°F. (Gas Mark 4) for about 2½–3 hours until uniformly hot. Remove the foil wrapping. Add bacon if not already included in the dish and sprinkle with fresh or frozen chopped parsley just before serving.

Bouquets garnis

Preparation. Pick stalks of parsley, strip off leaves, chop and freeze separately. To each stalk add 1 sprig of thyme and ½ a bay leaf—green leaves, if available. Tie the bouquets firmly in two places with white thread.

Freezing. Put the first bouquet horizontally in the bottom of a large polythene bag, fold the bag up and over from the bottom, place another bouquet and fold again, and so on until the bag is full and rolled right up. Overwrap in another polythene bag, seal and label.

To Use. Use the bouquets directly from the freezer, one or two at a time as required for chosen recipes.

Brandy in freezer cooking

See WINE.

Bread

Home-made or bakery bread will keep for many months in a polythene bag in a home freezer. Sliced bread can be frozen in its original wrapper and the slices toasted without thawing. Store opened package in a polythene bag to prevent drying. Home-made bread can be 'flash-baked'—cooked at a high oven temperature until rising is completed with the inactivation of the yeast, but the bread is not completely cooked. It can then be cooled, frozen, and the cooking completed at a later stage by putting the frozen, half-cooked loaf into a hot oven for about 40 minutes. Exact timing depends on the size of the loaf. A large, fully cooked loaf will take 4 or 5 hours to defrost at room temperature, but only about 40 minutes in a warming drawer or very slow oven. As bread is very bulky it should be stored in small quantities only for use in emergencies.

Bread sauce

For a freezer quantity of sauce, stick a large onion with a dozen cloves, put it in a pan with enough milk to cover and infuse on a low heat. Do not allow the milk to boil. After infusing, remove the onion and set aside. Add enough fresh or partly-thawed breadcrumbs to produce the desired creamy consistency (about 4 oz. per pint of milk), a little butter, salt and white pepper. Allow to become quite cold before freezing.

Freezing. Cut the onion into quarters, leaving in the cloves. Set one quarter in each waxed container—margarine cartons are ideal for bread sauce—and pour in the sauce. Leave a little HEADSPACE and replace the lids of the cartons. Seal.

Freezer Life. Up to 3 months.

To Use. Reheat the sauce in a double boiler or thick saucepan. When sufficiently thawed, remove the onion. When quite hot, remove from heat, add a large piece of butter and a little cream and beat well. Adjust seasoning.

Breadcrumbs

A large loaf of bread made into fine crumbs by means of a blender should be kept in a polythene bag in the freezer. If the bread was dry when crumbed, it will not freeze into a lump. New, moist bread should be lightly pounded inside its bag when half-frozen, to stop it from lumping together and thus being less easy to measure into usable quantities. When making BREAD SAUCE, allow crumbs to stand at room temperature before adding to the warm milk. It is possible that icy-cold crumbs will curdle the milk. Breadcrumbs have a freezer life of up to 1 year.

Breast of lamb

A fatty cut of meat that is better cooked and eaten than cooked and frozen. Uncooked breast of lamb can be kept for 3–4 months in the freezer but longer storage allows a rancid flavour and odour to develop.

Brisket

Not a good cut of meat for freezing as it has thick layers of fat and thin, lean strata. It should be used within 3 months. Freezing the cooked joint is not recommended.

Broad beans

See also GREEN PEAS. It is not advisable to buy broad beans from a town shop for freezing, or to freeze home-grown produce if the pods have grown large and tough.

Blanch young, tender beans for 3 minutes. Cool and drain and pack in wax cartons or polythene bags. Seal and label.

Freezer Life. Up to 1 year.

To Use. Cook in fast-boiling salted water for 7–10 minutes straight from the freezer.

Broccoli

Preparation. The green or purple shoots and tender top leaves of garden-grown broccoli should be washed and have any tough stalks discarded before BLANCHING for 3 minutes. Drain carefully.

Freezing. Put a layer of stalks gently into wax or polythene boxes, with tips all facing the same way, place double grease-proof or foil on top of first layer and arrange a second layer of broccoli with tips over stalks. Cover, seal and label.

Freezer Life. Up to 6 months.

To Use. Carefully remove as many spears as you need. Cook frozen broccoli direct from the freezer in a small quantity of fast-boiling, salted water, until the stalks are just tender when touched with a fork—not more than 10 or 12 minutes.

Brown sauce

This sauce can be made for the freezer in multiples of the basic quantity: 1 large carrot, 1 large onion, 2 small or 1 large stick of celery, 2 oz. flour, 2 pints of STOCK, 4 skinned and finely sliced tomatoes or their equivalent in TOMATO PURÉE (about 2 tablespoons) salt and pepper, a BOUQUET GARNI. Chop the vegetables finely and cook gently in olive oil until they are soft but not coloured. Sprinkle the flour over the vegetables and cook, stirring regularly, until the flour and oil have become a gravy-colour but the vegetables are still not burned. Add tomatoes or purée and the stock slowly, stirring all the time. Put in the bouquet and bring the mixture to the boil. Half-cover the pan and simmer the sauce until it is well reduced. Season. Strain and cool before freezing.

Freezing. Put the sauce in serving quantities in plastic or waxed containers, leaving HEADSPACE. Seal and label.

Freezer Life. Two or three months if frozen stock was used, up to 6 months if stock was freshly made.

To Use. Turn the required quantity of sauce into a double boiler, or thick saucepan. Break up the frozen mass when the outside begins to thaw, and if necessary add a little more stock or tomato purée. Taste for seasoning before serving and add about 2 tablespoons medium or sweet sherry for each pint of sauce.

Brussels sprouts

Preparation. Only home-grown sprouts repay the effort of freezing them. They are available during a six-month season in shops, and all the year round in ready-frozen packs. Small, firm sprouts should be picked for freezing while all the outer leaves are still tight. Wash, trim the stalks, and BLANCH for 4–6 minutes, depending on size of sprout. Cool and drain.

Freezing. Put the blanched sprouts, graded for size, into polythene bags and seal.

Freezer Life. Up to 1 year.

To Use. Cook the sprouts straight from the freezer in a small quantity of boiling, salted water for not more than 10 or 12 minutes.

Budgeting

It is easier to budget for freezer shopping by the month or even by the quarter, rather than by the week. If the weekly system has to be maintained, and it is not always easy to change it from a standing start, a float is gradually built up as the catering becomes freezer-orientated. For instance, buying large packs of frozen vegetables instead of small represents a significant saving over several weeks. Also, meat can be bought mid-week when the price is usually lower than at week-ends. In coastal areas, fish can be bought directly from the market or even occasionally, from incoming trawlers. Vegetables bought from a grower are far cheaper than those in shops, and are worth freezing, whereas shop-bought ones are not usually suitable for freezing. Over quite a short period, the savings amount to enough to cover BULK PURCHASES of meat and ready-frozen food, or seasonal fruit and vegetables which must be bought in quantity during a few summer weeks. After the first few months, and with a little applied discipline, freezer budgeting becomes self-balancing.

Bulk purchase	Buying ready-frozen food in bulk represents a freezer economy greater than any other, both in terms of money and expended effort. All items available from frozen food cabinets in shops—meat products, fish, confectionery, fruit and vegetables—can be obtained in large quantities, conveniently packed for freezing. Also, Birds Eye offer a specialized list of items for home freezers, including many of the classic haute cuisine dishes. Locally, butchers and private firms can often offer bulk supplies, and these may include regional items which are not nationally available. Bulk orders can usually be made by telephone, with payment on a cash-on-delivery basis. Also see BUDGETING, and MEAT, PURCHASE OF.
Butter	Left in its wrapping and overwrapped in a polythene bag, butter will keep for at least 6 weeks in the freezer. From the point of view of using space to best effect, however, butter should be considered as an emergency item and stored in small quantities, 1 lb. or 2 lb. only.
Butter-cream	A selection of coloured and flavoured butter-creams for cake filling or decoration can be kept in small plastic boxes in the freezer. They can be dug out in required quantities and worked with a fork when thawing to restore the smooth texture. Butter-based mixtures do not always freeze satisfactorily, but the high proportion of sugar in this mixture maintains it in good condition for weeks as it tends to delay the development of rancidity. *Freezer Life*. Up to 3 months.
Cabbage	Cabbage is obtainable at a reasonable price nearly all the year round, and is therefore not worth the time, trouble or space of freezing.
Cake icing	Home-made glacé and royal icing may not freeze and thaw satisfactorily on home-made cakes. It may crack and lift clear of the surface. But with careful handling glacé-iced cakes can usually be frozen successfully. Alternatively, cakes can be iced during the thawing period. Sponge cakes can be filled with butter cream. Similarly some shop-bought iced cakes may freeze successfully. Commercially-frozen éclairs are coated with melted chocolate rather than glacé icing and are therefore good freezer subjects.
Cake mixtures	*Preparation*. Victoria sponge or Madeira or fruit cake mixtures can be frozen uncooked if there is enough time to mix

91

them but not enough to bake them in the same session. Genoese sponges or those made by beating the egg whites and yolks separately are too fragile in construction to be frozen before cooking.

Freezing. Put the cake mixture into a greased and lined tin—or use the very convenient eight-inch paper cases which can be bought at stationery shops—cover the top of the mixture lightly with a piece of foil or greaseproof paper, and overwrap in a polythene bag. Stand the cake tins level in the freezer, to stop the contents heeling to one side.

Freezer Life. Up to 2 months.

To Use. Thaw the mixtures at room temperature in the tins and cook in the usual way.

Cakes

Freshly baked home-made or shop-bought sponge cakes, buns and Madeira cake will all freeze successfully. Cooked rich fruit cakes store equally well in tins and it is a waste of space to freeze them.

Freezing. Place cakes, decorated or not, in rigid polythene boxes, seal and label. To avoid drying during storage, select a box only a little larger than the cake(s) so that very little air remains in the sealed container. Removal of a large cake is facilitated if two strips of foil are crossed and placed beneath the cake.

Freezer Life. Up to 4 months—up to 3 months if BUTTER-CREAM is used.

To Use. Small fairy cakes or currant buns take about an hour to thaw at room temperature. Sponge or layer cakes need about 2 hours and Madeira or large decorated gateaux may take up to half a day for complete thawing.

Calabrese

This is a stubbier, less leafy form of broccoli, and is seldom found in shops. It is of a delicate flavour. Prepare, pack and freeze as BROCCOLI.

Canned food

Large cans of fruit, fruit and vegetable juices, frankfurters, skinless sausages intended for catering establishments, are occasionally available from wholesale grocers at economical prices. These may be opened, their contents divided into serving portions and frozen in appropriate containers. They can be taken to have a freezer life of 2 or 3 months for meat products, up to 6 months for fruit and juices. Some loss of texture may be noticed in some products.

Cannelloni

Preparation. For 2 people simmer 6 large tubes of cannelloni in plenty of salted water until just cooked. Lift from the pan on a fish slice or draining spoon, avoiding breakage. Cool slightly before handling. Prepare about 1¼ lb. of minced veal, beef or chicken, season with 1 clove of garlic (crushed), salt and pepper and a little marjoram, bind with a beaten egg. Frozen leftover meat should only be used if the cannelloni is to be cooked and eaten immediately. Fill the tubes with the meat mixture, using a forcing bag or small polythene bag with a corner cut off. Thaw appropriate quantity of TOMATO PURÉE, thin to pouring consistency with STOCK, taste for seasoning.

Freezing. Lay the cannelloni in serving quantities in foil-lined shallow oven dishes. Push the meat-filled tubes well down into tomato sauce, cover the dishes with extra foil and freeze, keeping the dish level. When the contents are solid, remove foil package, cover closely with spare foil, overwrap in a polythene bag, seal and label.

Freezer Life. Up to 6 months, as long as fresh meat is used.

To Use. Allow foil package to thaw at room temperature for about 1 hour, until the foil can be peeled off. Place the frozen block in a thick saucepan and heat carefully until thoroughly hot. Remove cannelloni and place on serving dish. Thicken the tomato sauce with a little flour and pour over cannelloni. If liked, pour over about ¼ pint thawed white sauce, sprinkle with grated Parmesan cheese and brown in the oven at 400° F. (Gas Mark 6) for 15–20 minutes.

Carbonnade of beef

Preparation. For 4 portions. Trim 1½ lb. chuck steak and cut into cubes. Peel and slice 2 onions. Chop and crush 1 clove garlic with a little salt. Heat about 4 tablespoons of oil in a large casserole and quickly brown the meat on all sides. Lower the heat and cook onions until lightly browned. Stir in 1 oz. flour and then add ½ pint of brown ale and 1 pint of water. Add crushed garlic and fresh or frozen BOUQUET GARNI and season with salt, pepper and 1 teaspoon of wine vinegar. Cover the casserole and cook in the oven at 325° F. (Gas Mark 3) for 2 hours. Spread two ¼-inch thick slices of crustless bread with plenty of French mustard and cut each slice diagonally into 4 triangles. Remove casserole from oven and cool rapidly by running cold water over the closely lidded container.

Freezing. When cool, place carbonnade in a foil-lined ovenproof casserole and arrange the bread on top, mustard side uppermost. Push each piece below the surface to ensure that the bread is completely soaked in gravy. Cover casserole with another piece of foil and freeze. Overwrap in a polythene bag, seal and label.

Freezer Life. Up to 3 months.

To Use. Remove foil package from polythene bag, place in ovenproof dish and heat at 425°F. (Gas Mark 7) for about 1 hour, removing the foil when food has begun to thaw. Then raise heat to 450°F. (Gas Mark 8) for $\frac{1}{2}$ hour or until the topping is browned and crisp.

Carrots

Preparation. Only very new, garden-grown carrots repay the effort of freezing. Pull them when they are no more than middle-finger length, cut off greenery, wash and rub off the skin with a brush or peel after blanching and cooling. The carrots should be small enough to be frozen whole. BLANCH for 5 minutes.

Freezing. Put the cooled, drained carrots into polythene bags without HEADSPACE, seal. Lay the bags flat inside the freezer until the vegetables are solidly frozen, to avoid breakage. Then pack vegetables closely. Seal and label.

Freezer Life. Up to 1 year.

To Use. Cook the carrots directly from the freezer in a small quantity of boiling, salted water for no more than 10 or 12 minutes, or reheat in a covered dish in the oven with butter and a pinch of fresh or frozen mixed herbs.

Casing

The outside case of a home freezer is often made of stove enamel, or laminated plastic, highly resistant to stains and chipping, but not to continuous damp. The outer casing should be cleaned regularly with mild detergent, dried and occasionally polished with silicone cream. But care should be taken not to allow detergent or cream to come into contact with the inner casing.

Casseroles

Preparation. Meat or poultry cooked in a casserole, either humbly for daily meals or magnificently with wine for festivities, can be prepared in large quantities, cooked and frozen in serving portions. See WINE. Pork should not be considered if the dish is to be stored for more than 6 weeks. Similarly ham and bacon in pieces, rolls or slices. See individual entries. Overcooking must be avoided, and the dish should contain plenty of gravy or sauce to cover the meat and completely avoid drying during storage. Root vegetables,

94

other than onions, should be added to the dish when the meat is already partly cooked, so that they will not develop a reheated flavour or turn to mush on reheating. Casserole dishes with sliced potatoes on the top should not be browned during first cooking. Cool the food thoroughly, either by standing a metal cooking pot in cold water, or turning the contents into a bowl standing it in cold water. Skim off excess fat before freezing and freeze as soon as the food has cooled to room temperature.

Freezing. Line an ovenproof dish with foil and freeze the food inside the foil. When the food is solidly frozen, take out the frozen package, overwrap tightly with a polythene bag, seal and label clearly with contents and date. Or the food can be turned out of its cooking dish into a plastic box or bowl and sealed, leaving HEADSPACE.

Freezer Life. No more than 6 weeks if bacon, ham or pork is included, up to 3 months for dishes with much oil and wine, 4–6 months for plain dishes.

To Use. Put the food in foil packages back into the serving dishes directly from the freezer, reheat in a slow oven with a watch kept for possible drying of the gravy. Remove the foil when the food starts to thaw, putting it over the top of the dish as an extra protection against drying. Food frozen in plastic boxes is tipped out into the cooking dish and reheated in the same way. Potato topping should be browned during reheating.

Cassoulet

Preparation. An immense, very rich party dish with a short but worthwhile freezer life. To prepare enough for 16 people: $1\frac{1}{2}$ lb. of haricot beans, soaked and half-cooked in a mixture of STOCK and water, with a bay leaf but no salt, 8 oz. of belly pork, 6 cloves of garlic, crushed or chopped, half-shoulder or top half of a leg of lamb, a small duck, jointed, and/or half a smoked or pickled goose—difficult to obtain except in specialist shops, but worth looking for. Also, some beef dripping with its jelly, 6 oz. of chipolata sausage, 8 tablespoons of TOMATO PURÉE, salt, black pepper, a large BOUQUET GARNI and a breakfast-cupful of brown or wholemeal breadcrumbs, to be added during final cooking. Drain the cooked beans and reserve the liquor. Cut the lamb into large chunks and fry with the duck joints in the dripping, in one very large or two smaller stew pans. Add the pork in one piece, or in half for two pans, the beans with most of their liquor, the garlic and bouquet, a little salt and plenty of black pepper.

Cover and cook very slowly for about 1¼ hours. Top up with the bean liquor from time to time as necessary. Meanwhile, put the tomato purée in a thick saucepan with a little salt, pepper and a pinch of sugar. Heat gently to thaw. When the bean mixture has been cooking for about 1½ hours, put in the goose (if used) cut into joints. Half an hour later, add the sausages. After a further hour of cooking, take out the duck and the pork, cut into large pieces—remove most of the fat and put back with the beans. Mix the tomato pulp carefully through the whole mass in the pan. Divide the enormous mixture into two or three bowls, cool by standing the bowls in cold water with ice cubes, chill in the refrigerator before freezing.

Freezing. Freeze the cassoulet in two or three foil-lined ovenproof casseroles—to freeze all in one dish would take too long both in freezing and thawing—covered with extra foil. Remove the foil packages when the contents are solidly frozen, overwrap in polythene bags, seal and label.

Freezer Life. Up to 2 weeks only since it is assumed that such a dish will be prepared for a party and would be altogether too much to make on the day.

To Use. Stand the cassoulet in its freezer wrappings in the refrigerator overnight. If two casseroles are used, the total heating time will be about 4 hours. If three are used, this will be about 3 hours. Take the cassoulet from the freezer and replace in the casseroles. Cover and heat at 425° F. (Gas Mark 7). After 2 or 3 hours (depending on the number of casseroles which are used), remove the lids and the foil covering. Adjust the seasoning and cover the top of the meat with the breadcrumbs. Brown the topping in the oven. Guard carefully against drying.

Cauliflower

Preparation. Only garden-grown cauliflowers are worth freezing in sprigs, or whole if they are small and tender with a hood of small, pale green leaves over the curd. Wash and pull off sprigs before BLANCHING for 3 minutes.

Freezing. Pack most tenderly, and preferably in polythene or waxed containers, to protect frozen cauliflower from assault by heavy freezer-neighbours, because cauliflower is best cooked from frozen and damage will not be apparent until after cooking. Interleave with foil or polythene.

To Use. Cook cauliflower direct from the freezer in fast-boiling, salted water for only as long as necessary to make the stalks tender.

Centigrade or Celsius	An accepted measurement of temperature in which 0° denotes freezing point and 100° the boiling point of water, under normal atmospheric pressure.
Cheese	*Preparation*. Cream or cottage cheese does not freeze well for long periods, becoming yellowish, hard and crumbly—but both are satisfactory for at least 6 weeks. Likewise the blue cheeses—Stilton, Roquefort, Danish Blue. The most practicable, and most useful cheese for freezing is Cheddar. This varies in price over the year, and should be bought in quantity at its lowest price. Cut a large piece into pound or half-pound wedges.
	Freezing. Wrap the cheese very closely, each wedge in a small polythene bag sealed with a plastic-covered wire tie or fastened with sticky tape. Overwrap four or five pieces at a time in another larger polythene bag and seal.
	Freezer Life. 4–6 months, but only 6 weeks for blue, cottage and cream cheeses. Cheshire, Edam and Caerphilly also freeze well. A few pounds of frozen grated Cheddar cheese is also very useful and keeps well for 4–6 months.
	To Use. Take out the required amount and leave in a covered box or cheese dish in the refrigerator, where it will quickly thaw ready to be used as freshly-bought. Be sure the cheese is completely thawed before it is eaten otherwise the flavour will be weak.
Cheese sauce	Grated Cheddar or a mixture of Cheddar or Gruyère and Parmesan cheese are added to frozen WHITE SAUCE, partly thawed in advance, and reheated but not boiled while the cheese melts. The whole sauce can be made and frozen, but Gruyère cheese should not be used in this case—it may become stringy during freezing. About 5 oz. of grated Cheddar cheese per pint gives a good flavour. If separation occurs during reheating, beat the sauce briskly with a wooden spoon.
	Freezer Life. Up to 6 months.
	To Use. Heat the sauce in a double boiler, so that it does not boil. If boiling does occur the texture of the cheese sauce is very granular.
Cherries	*Preparation*. Only the large, red varieties are worth freezing, unless cherries are a particular favourite, in which case 'white' cherries or the sharp Morello are worth looking for and may be frozen. All stone fruit should, ideally, be pitted before freezing, or a bitter flavour develops in the flesh around the

97

stone. They *can* be frozen unpitted, but the freezer life will be shortened. Cherries should be stalked, stoned, washed under running cold water and drained. They benefit from being frozen in a 30% or 40% sugar SYRUP. The syrup is boiled and allowed to become quite cold before the fruit is added.

Freezing. Pour cold syrup into plastic or waxed containers to the half-way mark, and press the cherries well down into the container to exclude air bubbles. Keep submerged with crushed greaseproof paper. Seal the containers and stand them upright in the freezer until fruit and syrup are solidly frozen. The containers should not leak, but they might unless they are kept upright.

Freezer Life. Up to 1 year if the cherries have been stoned, 6 months if the stones are left in the fruit.

To Use. Leave the containers in the refrigerator overnight, turning the fruit out on to a covered dish to complete thawing at room temperature. If the fruit is to be cooked, it can be used directly from the freezer.

Chest-type freezers

A chest-type freezer has a hinged lid which lifts up from the top, and the contents are packed as in a box. Large chest-types are fitted with baskets to contain the upper layers of stored food, which are easily lifted out or moved along the upper ledge of the chest for the lower packages to be reached. When choosing a freezer, the size and reach of the potential user is an important consideration. A short person may not be able to reach the bottom of the chest easily, and will be better served by an UPRIGHT model, see separate entry.

Chicken

Ready-frozen chickens should be put into a home freezer as soon as practicable after purchase—never left at room temperature, or unwrapped. The shop wrapping should be overwrapped with a polythene bag, and sealed. Fresh fowls should be drawn, wiped clean, and the giblets put in a separate polythene bag. The feet should be removed and the shanks wrapped in polythene so that the sharp bones will not puncture the outer polythene bag. *Chickens should not be stuffed before freezing.* Jointing should be done before freezing. Pack in thick, gusseted polythene bags, pressing out all air pockets with the flat of the hand, and seal tightly with a plastic covered wire tie. Place packages at the bottom of a chest-type freezer, or against the walls of an upright model, where the temperature is lowest. A whole chicken must be thawed completely before cooking. Jointed birds should be allowed 3 or 4 hours, depending on size. Thawing can be hastened by putting the bird in its freezer wrapping under running *cold* water. Subsequent cooking should be done gently and thoroughly. Fresh chickens, frozen without stuffing, have a freezer life of up to 10 months.

Chinese beans   Never seen in shops, these blue-coloured beans turn green on cooking. Prepare, pack and freeze as HARICOTS VERTS.

Chips   Buy ready-frozen chips in 5 lb. bags from a bulk supplier. If you grow your own potatoes you may wish to prepare chips or game chips for the freezer at home. Potatoes should be sliced and steam blanched for two minutes then dried and oil blanched at 340°F. for 1 minute. Cool, freeze on a cake rack and pack in polythene bags—seal and label.
Freezer Life. Up to 6 months.
To Use. Deep fry straight from the freezer at 360°F. for about 2 minutes until thoroughly hot and golden brown.

Chops   Chops should be frozen in individual small polythene bags before packing together in larger bags, or each piece of meat separated from the next by a double layer of foil, cellophane or greaseproof paper. No more than half a dozen chops should be frozen in any one package, placed close to the walls of the freezer for quick freezing. After freezing, the packages can be stacked conveniently. Ideally the meat should be left to thaw in its freezer wrapping in the refrigerator overnight. Chops cooked direct from the freezer must be started off under gentle heat or they may be raw on the inside when the outside appears cooked. When the meat feels tender to the touch, the heat can be increased to brown the surface.
Freezer Life. Up to 3 months for pork, 6 months for lamb.

Choux pastry   *Preparation*. It is advised in cookery books that cream buns and éclairs should not be made in greater quantity than is immediately required. This does not apply to freezer owners. Prepare the pastry in multiples of any favoured recipe—given quantities of flour to water vary widely, and only experience shows which recipe suits an individual hand—only remembering to stir the flour *quickly* into the hot water and fat, leaving beating until the eggs are added. Overmixing in the first stage may prevent the pastry from rising. Pipe cream bun or éclair shapes on to a non-stick baking sheet or non-stick baking paper on an ordinary tray, cook, and cool on a wire tray, splitting each bun to let out the steam. Allow to become quite cold before freezing, but not to stand over-long exposed to air. Fill with whipped cream (38%–40% butter fat) and cover with melted chocolate.

Freezing. Pack the buns side by side in layers in a plastic box, with a piece of foil between successive layers. Seal and label adding 'with care'.

To Use. Leave buns at room temperature for about 1 hour.

Combination refrigerator-freezer

A two-door upright model with a compartment for freezing food from room temperature and a refrigerator above or below it. A useful appliance if floor space is limited and requirements for refrigerator and freezer space are small. The freezer part is not a large version of the frozen food storage compartment of a refrigerator. Its temperature can be lowered below $-18°$ C. ($0°$ F.) and has sufficient refrigeration capacity for the fast freezing of newly introduced foods.

Conservators

A refrigerated chest used in shops for storage of ice-cream and sometimes commercially-frozen foods at temperatures between $-18°$ C. and $-20°$ C. Not usually suitable for freezing fresh food from room temperature, as the refrigeration capacity may be insufficient to hold a temperature below $-18°$ C. ($0°$ F.) when fresh food is introduced, and not to be considered if offered second-hand in the guise of a home freezer.

Cooling

All cooked food or blanched vegetables *must* be cooled thoroughly to room temperature before being put into the freezer. A warm dish or package may raise the temperature inside the freezer to an undesirable level, will almost certainly warm the surface of any already frozen food with which it comes into contact, and the contents will not freeze satisfactorily. Food cooked in a tightly-lidded metal pan or stewpot can be left to stand in the sink with the cold water running over and round it until the contents have cooled. The contents of an earthenware cooking pot can be turned into an oven-glass or plastic bowl and stood in a large bowl of cold water containing ice cubes. Food should not be *cooled* in the refrigerator, but cooled food in its freezer container may, if necessary, be refrigerated for up to 2 hours before freezing.

Corn-on-the-cob

Preparation. Sweet corn should usually be considered as a bulk-purchase item, ready-frozen. Shop-bought corn should never be frozen. Home-grown cobs can be picked when small and tender, the silk barely green. Remove husk and silk, grade for size and BLANCH for 6 to 10 minutes according to size. To freeze corn kernels, cook the husked cobs in boiling water for 4 minutes, cool and drain. Cut the kernels off the cob if desired.

Freezing. Wrap whole cobs in foil, overwrap in polythene bags. Pack kernels in polythene bags or plastic or waxed containers.

Freezer Life. Up to 1 year.

To Use. Cook corn directly from the freezer. Whole cobs should be put into enough fast-boiling salted water to cover, and cooked until the kernels are just tender. Kernels should be cooked for 4 or 5 minutes in fast-boiling water.

Courgettes

Preparation. Choose courgettes of roughly equal size, no more than 4 or 5 inches long. Wash, but do not peel. Top and tail, if necessary. Cut the smallest courgettes in half lengthways, leaving the seeds. Larger specimens can be cut into $\frac{1}{2}$-inch slices. Steam over boiling water for 5 minutes. Turn them gently into a bowl, taking care to avoid breaking the softened pieces, and cool in a larger bowl of cold water.

Freezing. Freeze cut and sliced courgettes separately, in plastic or waxed containers, with HEADSPACE. Freeze in serving quantities, or in individual quantities which can be used according to need.

Freezer Life. Up to 1 year.

To Use. Turn the courgettes out of containers into a bowl, cover tightly with a lid or foil, reheat in a steamer pan. When they are hot, add plenty of butter, salt and pepper before serving. Courgettes frozen and thawed at room temperature can be served cold with a French dressing, or as an ingredient in RATATOUILLE.

Cream

Single cream is unsuitable for the freezer as it will separate. Whipping cream and double cream will freeze successfully if they are whipped beforehand. (Take care not to overwhip.) Unwhipped whipping or double cream may separate on thawing but the higher the butter fat content the better the chance of success. A little sugar stirred into the cream before freezing will help, as will gentle stirring after thawing.

Crumpets

Shop-bought crumpets can be frozen in a polythene bag and toasted directly from the freezer.

Cubic feet

The unit used to measure the capacity of home freezers, referring to the inside measurements. Also providing a rule-

101

of-thumb method of choosing a home freezer, allowing 3 or 4 cubic foot per member of the family. One cubic foot of space *may* contain up to 20 lb. of regular-shaped frozen food packs.

Cucumber

Cucumber is comprised largely of water, and cannot be frozen successfully in the raw state. The only possible exception to the rule of not freezing it is when it is contained in small cubes in a chilled soup or puréed in a soup or sauce.

Curry

Preparation. Any kind of curried meat or poultry—not pork, unless storage is going to be short-term, not fish or eggs— can be cooked and frozen. Seasoning is a matter of taste, and has to be decided by trial and error. Curry paste gives a better flavour than curry powder, but home-made curry powder with freshly-bought ingredients from an Oriental emporium is best of all. This is not as troublesome as it may sound because the ingredients are already ground, and it is an interesting exercise which soon becomes a habit. Cool the curry before freezing, by standing a metal cooking pot in a bowl of cold water, or by turning the food into a bowl and standing the bowl in cold water. If there is any excess fat, remove it before freezing.

Freezing. Freeze curry in serving quantities. Freeze the food in a foil-lined serving dish, taking out the foil package when the contents are solidly frozen and overwrapping in a polythene bag. Exclude all air, seal very tightly indeed, and label clearly. If the curry is turned out of the serving dish and frozen in a plastic bowl or box, seal the edges of the box with sticky tape, and label.

Freezer Life. 3–4 months.

To Use. Reheat the curry in a covered serving dish in a slow oven, or in a pan over gentle heat, stirring regularly and gently. Do not allow the sauce to reduce too much. Serve with RICE and DAHL, bananas in lemon juice, poppadums, diced cucumber, yoghurt, and chutney or other suitable accompaniments according to taste.

Curry sauce

Preparation. A rich, well-flavoured curry sauce can be made in quantity for the freezer from the basic proportions which produce about 1½ pints of sauce. A large, strong onion, thinly sliced, 2 tablespoons oil, 4 skinned and roughly chopped tomatoes, 3 cloves of crushed garlic, 2 teaspoons of curry paste, or more to taste, small piece of root ginger, scraped and shredded, salt, 1 oz. flour, ½ pint chicken stock. Fry the onion in the oil, but do not brown. Put in the curry

102

paste and cook, stirring for 2 or 3 minutes. Add tomatoes and garlic, salt and ginger. Simmer for about 15 minutes, or until the sauce looks and smells very rich. Sprinkle on the flour. Stir and cook for 2 minutes. Add stock gradually and simmer for 10 minutes, cool before freezing.

Freezing. Put the sauce in serving quantities in waxed or plastic containers, leaving HEADSPACE. Seal and label.

Freezer Life. Up to 4 months.

To Use. Turn the sauce out of containers into a small pan, break up with a fork when beginning to thaw, stir to avoid scorching. Mix with or pour over leftover meat cubes, etc. Adjust seasoning.

Dahl

Preparation. To be served with CURRY, dahl is made for freezing in multiples of the basic quantity: 8 oz. red lentils, one medium onion chopped, 2 or 3 tablespoons of curry powder or paste, stock, 2 oz. butter and salt. Put the lentils in a bowl and cover with boiling water. Leave to stand for about 1 hour. Put them, drained, into a thick pan, add the chopped onion, butter, curry powder or paste, and STOCK to cover. Bring to the boil, reduce heat and simmer for about $\frac{1}{2}$ hour. Add salt to taste, and continue until the mixture has the appearance of a purée and is beginning to 'break' or separate. Cool before freezing.

Freezing. Put dahl in serving quantities in waxed or plastic containers, or in polythene bags to be frozen in 1 lb. sugar cartons, leaving HEADSPACE. Seal and label.

Freezer Life. Up to 6 months.

To Use. Reheat dahl in a saucepan, stirring regularly once thawing has begun, or put in a covered dish in the oven.

Damp

A home freezer should never be placed in a damp situation. The casing may rust and the electrical and mechanical parts may be affected adversely.

Deep freezing

A *commercial* process involving the cooling of food by blasts of air at ultra-low temperature, $-73°$C. ($-100°$F.).

Defrosting

A home freezer of the CHEST TYPE should not need to be defrosted more than twice a year. But this depends on usage. UPRIGHT models may have to be treated more frequently, since they may build up more frost. A great deal of frost collecting round door or lid is an indication of a poor seal and action should be taken to remedy the poor fit. Frost should be removed frequently with a wooden or plastic spatula—

metal may crack or break the casing and damage the cooling pipes. Full defrosting should be carried out when stocks of frozen food are low, and any remaining packages can be stored in the refrigerator for a few hours. Switch off the electric current, remove plug and place bowls or buckets of hot water inside the freezer. Leave the door or lid open until all the frost has loosened sufficiently for it to be scraped away with the chosen implement. Wash inside and out with warm water or a solution of 1 tablespoon of bicarbonate of soda to 4 pints of water. Dry with a soft cloth. Switch on the current, and close the freezer door or lid. After an hour or two, replace the packages. See also CASING.

Domestic refrigerator

An appliance for the short-term storage of non-frozen foods, often with a small compartment intended for storage of commercially quick-frozen food for a time dictated by the STAR MARKING on the door of the compartment and on the food packaging. It is not recommended that foods be frozen in such a compartment unless it is a genuine food freezing compartment.

Doughnuts

Preparation. Ready-frozen doughnuts are obtainable from bulk suppliers. Shop-bought doughnuts, if known to be light and good, can be stored in a home freezer. The home-made variety are made in quantity to any favoured recipe and cooled before freezing.

Freezing. Put the doughnuts in usable quantities—6 or 8—in polythene bags. Expel all air and seal with a plastic-covered wire tie. Several small bags can be overwrapped and sealed in one large bag.

Freezer Life. 2–3 months.

To Use. Put the doughnuts into a very slow oven or warming drawer for about 20 minutes.

Dried skim milk

With its reduced fat content, dried skim milk can produce better results than whole milk in sauces and cream soup for the freezer, with less risk of the mixture separating during freezing and having to be beaten smooth on reheating. Single or double cream can be stirred into the mixture before serving.

Dry freezing

This refers to fruit frozen without sugar or syrup.

Duck

Pack, freeze and thaw as for CHICKENS. The so-called 'Aylesbury' duck has a freezer life of 4–6 months. Wild duck, taken from river or marsh, should be hung before being drawn for a slightly shorter period than would be employed if the bird were not to be frozen.

Eggs

Preparation. Lightly beat whole fresh eggs with a good pinch of salt or sugar to prevent thickening. Do not beat egg whites if they are to be frozen separate from the yolks. Stir, but do not beat, yolks to be frozen alone adding a good pinch of salt or sugar.

Freezing. Put beaten whole egg into an ice-cube tray and store the frozen blocks, or freeze in half-dozen quantities in a plastic bowl. Freeze separated whites in waxed cartons, separated yolks in the ice-cube tray. Label according to addition of salt or sugar. Hard-boiled eggs develop a leathery texture in the whites when frozen and should not be put into the freezer as they stand or included in pies, curry, sandwiches, etc.

Freezer Life. 4–6 months.

To Use. Thaw whole eggs and separated yolks at room temperature for an hour, or warm gently in a bowl over warm water. Three tablespoons of whole egg mixture equals one egg, two spoons of white and one of yolk if they are separated. Separately frozen whites can be broken up, thawed and beaten in one operation in a mixer for making meringues.

Enzymes

An enzyme is described as 'an organic catalyst'—a naturally-occurring substance with the power to accelerate chemical reactions while itself remaining unaltered. In terms of food, this means that the activity of enzymes which exist in all animal and vegetable substances will, in the long run, bring about undesirable changes in the tissues. The blanching of vegetables destroys enzyme activity before freezing. The freezing process itself slows down the activity in other foods to a marked degree. The temperature in a home freezer is not low enough to eliminate enzymic changes completely. During long storage beyond the periods recommended such changes reduce the palatability of food but they do *not* constitute a health hazard.

Escalopes of veal

Preparation. Escalopes of veal which are to be egg-and-breadcrumbed for frying, or sprinkled with finely chopped herbs and briefly fried in butter, should not be cooked before freezing. Beat the escalopes out, or have it done by the butcher, and freeze uncooked. For cooking and freezing escalopes, chop an onion finely and soften it in margarine, then place the escalopes in the pan with the onions under and round them, and cook gently until the meat begins to turn colour. *Do not overcook*. Remove the meat from the pan, pour a glass or more of white wine or sherry, according to the number of escalopes being cooked, over the onions and juice and bubble the mixture for a minute. Stir in an appropriate quantity of flour, cook, and add white stock to make a creamy sauce. Season with salt, pepper and a clove or two of crushed garlic. Remove the pan from the heat, replace the escalopes in the sauce. If the cooking pan has a lid, replace it and cool the meat in the pan under running cold water. If a frying pan was used, turn meat and sauce into a bowl and stand it in a bowl of cold water containing ice-cubes, if possible.

Freezing. Put the meat and the sauce in serving quantities in foil baking dishes or in a foil-lined ovenproof dish, covering the meat completely with the sauce. Cover the dish with an extra piece of foil, freeze and overwrap in a polythene bag, seal and label.

Freezer Life. 4–6 months.

To Use. Leave escalopes in sauce in freezer containers in the refrigerator overnight. Remove the escalopes and put them on a plate and cover. Turn sauce into a thick frying pan or stew pan. Heat the sauce, but do not allow it to boil. Blend a small carton or more of single cream, according to the prepared quantity of sauce, into the mixture and stir until all is heated. Replace the meat and continue reheating over a gentle heat until the escalopes are hot. Thaw frozen raw escalopes and coat in egg and breadcrumbs in the usual way.

Fahrenheit

An accepted measurement of temperature in which 32° denotes freezing point and 212° the boiling point of water, under normal atmospheric pressure.

Fish

Preparation. Only very fresh fish indeed should be put into a home freezer. Because fish can only truly be called 'fresh' for a few hours after leaving the water, this effectively cuts out for freezer purposes any fish bought from an inland fishmonger. In these circumstances commercially quick-frozen fish is the answer. Fish undergoes a rapid process of AUTOLYSIS. Newly-caught fish, or that bought from an irreproachable seaside fishmonger, is gutted, trimmed, washed and dried. Fish may be frozen with a savoury stuffing, topping or sauce.

Freezing. Cutlets or pieces of whole small fish are frozen with foil between pieces and overwrapped in a thick polythene bag, tightly sealed with a plastic-covered wire tie at the neck. Fish, with or without stuffing, can be frozen in foil inside its ovenproof cooking dish, when frozen the foil package can be removed and overwrapped tightly with polythene.

Freezer Life. 2–3 months for oily fish—herrings, halibut, turbot. Fish such as cod, haddock, plaice, has a freezer life of up to 4 months. Trout—2 months.

To Use. Fish is cooked from the frozen condition, allowing enough extra cooking time for the centre to be completely thawed and cooked.

See also 'FISH—LEFTOVERS'.

Fish—leftovers

Preparation. Leftover fish can be flaked and mixed with freshly mashed potatoes and seasoning for fish cakes or fish pie. It is important that the cooked fish should be made up and frozen as soon as possible after first cooking. The cooked fish or the prepared dish must not be left to stand at room temperature or kept more than 1–2 hours in the refrigerator before freezing.

Freezing. Put uncooked fish cakes between double squares of foil, overwrap in a polythene bag, seal, label. Fish pie prepared in a foil baking dish ready for cooking should be covered with a piece of foil, overwrapped in polythene, sealed and labelled.

Freezer Life. Up to 1 month.

To Use. Fry fish cakes in hot fat straight from the freezer. Leave foil cover on fish pie until thawed through in a moderate oven, remove cover for browning.

Flies

The house fly, blow fly and bluebottle are the enemies of any food handler. They should be treated in the same way by freezer owners and non-freezer owners—viz. keep food covered to prevent flies coming into contact with it.

Foil dishes

Pudding bowls, baking dishes, individual pie dishes, small fruit pie plates and patty pans are obtainable in packets from most large stationer's shops or hardware stores, and have many applications for the home freezer. Foil pie dishes and plates do not require greasing before being lined with pastry, though the individual dishes used for YORKSHIRE PUD-DINGS should be lightly smeared with vegetable oil before the batter is poured in. Acid fruits and tomatoes should not be placed directly on foil unless it has a protective coating. Such foods may react with the foil.

Free-running packs

Most vegetables bought in bulk are 'free running'—meaning that the peas, beans, sprouts or mixed vegetables will be loose inside the bag, not solidly packed. The loose packing means that the required quantity can be measured exactly before cooking. Home-frozen vegetables should be packed loosely during freezing and when frozen, packed more compactly.

Freezer burn

A term applied to the greyish-white marks on the surface of poultry, meat or fish that has not been properly wrapped before freezing, also may occur in frozen foods which are stored for a very long time. The marks are caused by dehydration, and will not occur if all freezer packages are rendered as air-tight as possible and firmly sealed. See also PACKAGING FOR THE FREEZER, and SEALING. Ice crystals in the outer layers of foods may be converted to water vapour and the surface, particularly of meat, become dry and tough.

Freezer hire

Private firms offering bulk supplies of ready-frozen food will often offer home-freezers on extended hire. This arrangement will usually have the benefit of a built-in maintenance contract, but the hire charges offset the lower costs of the food. Hiring is only a good economic proposition under particular circumstances—if a household moves about the country, having to clear the freezer at every move, if it is felt that a freezer would only be useful for part of every year, if the capital outlay on buying a freezer is too great, or as a trial run before investing.

Freezer life or High Quality life

A term used to denote the maximum recommended length of time for which any item can be stored in a freezer before it obviously begins to lose colour, flavour or texture. Fat meat and fish have a comparatively short 'freezer life'—bread, fruit, cakes, pastry and most vegetables have a 'freezer life' of between 6 months and 1 year. See individual items.

French beans

Preparation. Do not freeze French beans bought in a town shop, because they will have been picked at least 24 hours earlier and thus be beyond the point where the frozen result will be successful. Home or garden grown French beans should be picked when small, very young and very crisp. Top and tail the beans, discarding any which feel too soft or too hard. Beans for freezing should be small enough not to need slicing. BLANCH for 3 minutes.

Freezing. Pack the frozen beans loosely into polythene

108

bags, tie and freeze. When frozen, pack the beans more compactly and re-tie polythene bag, label.

Freezer Life. Up to 1 year.

To Use. Cook the beans directly from the freezer in a little fast-boiling salted water, for no more than 7–10 minutes.

French flan pastry

Preparation. See also PASTRY. This rich pastry can be difficult to roll at any time. To reduce the possibility of failure through cracking or crumbling, it should be frozen ready for cooking, on a foil pie-plate with or without a fruit filling. Make in multiples of the basic quantity for one eight-inch pie: 4 oz. plain flour, 2 oz. butter, 2 oz. castor sugar, 2 egg yolks, 2 drops vanilla essence or a pinch of powdered cinnamon. Sift the flour with a small pinch of salt on to a pastry board, make a well in the centre and put the other ingredients into it. Using the tips of the fingers—previously rubbed with an ice-cube—work the egg yolks into the butter and sugar. Draw the flour inwards from the top of the 'well', and mix it with the rest as quickly as possible, giving the paste no opportunity to become sticky. Knead quickly and lightly until the paste is smooth, then pat into a square and put directly into the freezer, without wrapping. After 15 to 20 minutes, take the paste from the freezer and roll it lightly but firmly to shape, using the minimum number of movements with the rolling pin to avoid stretching and tearing the pastry. Lift one edge of the paste on the rolling pin and set it down into an oiled flan ring set in a large foil pie plate. Let the paste drop into the ring, and cut it by rolling firmly over the top edge of the ring, if the pastry is to be frozen before cooking. If the pie is to be filled and frozen, do not cut the pastry but put in the filling—blackcurrants, apples or plums cooked almost to a purée with sugar, either fresh or frozen—turn the overlapping pastry across the filling and cut it to lie in leaves across the top, with a hole in the middle. Cool pastry and filling before freezing.

Freezing. Freeze flan cases with additional support under the foil pie dish—a cake board, or the lid of a plastic box or biscuit box or biscuit tin—until solidly frozen. Treat filled pies in the same way, do not handle again until frozen solid. Put frozen cases or pies into plastic boxes, setting them on two crossed strips of folded foil with the ends above the surface of the pies, to act as a handle for lifting. Seal and label 'with care'.

Freezer Life. Up to 4 months.

To Use. Fill empty flan cases and cook directly from

109

freezer. Cook filled pies directly from freezer, in a moderate oven. The pastry should be biscuit-coloured, but never browned. Great care must be taken in cooking that the pastry does not scorch.

Frost

A thick coating of frost often forms in the top twelve inches of a chest-type home freezer, and its effect is to reduce the freezer's efficiency. Accumulations of frost should be scraped off regularly with a wooden or plastic spatula—not a metal implement, which can easily damage the freezer wall or even the cooling pipes behind it. Check that the ice-formation is not caused by an inefficient lid or door seal.

Frozen food storage compartment

The section of a household refrigerator designed for the storage of quick-frozen foods. Frozen food compartments maintain a maximum temperature of about $-18°$ C. ($0°$ F.), $-12°$ C ($10°$ F.) or $-6°$ C. ($21°$ F.) indicated by the number of stars on the compartment's door, but also dependent on the thermostat setting. See also STAR MARKING.

Fruit pies

Preparation. Fruit-filled pies survive storage in better shape if they are frozen raw. Cooked pastry is delicate, and a ready-cooked pie most susceptible to accidental squashing in the freezer. Pies are best prepared in foil pie plates or dishes. Pies with no pastry underneath should be frozen in foil dishes manufactured with protective coating or acid in the fruit may react with the aluminium foil. The tops of covered pies should be pricked with a fork before freezing, or have cuts made to let out the steam during baking. The pastry may crack if the piercing is done after freezing.

Freezing. Put pies in their dishes inside polythene bags and seal the bags with plastic-covered wire ties. Stand the dishes level inside the freezer until pastry and filling are solidly frozen.

Freezer Life. According to the pie filling, usually 4–6 months.

To Use. Pies can be cooked immediately after being taken from the freezer, in their foil dishes. Sprinkle with sugar. Cook at an oven temperature suitable for the pastry, reducing the heat when the pastry is well-risen and extending the cooking time slightly to make sure that the filling is properly thawed and cooked.

Fruit tarts

Preparation. Freshly cooked or already-frozen sliced or puréed fruit—well sweetened—can be filled into pastry-lined foil pie plates or dishes and frozen raw or cooked. Small tartlets with fruit filling are liable to be damaged during storage, and are better prepared by thawing filling and pastry immediately before use. Cooked tarts and fillings must be cooled before freezing.

Freezing. Put uncooked tarts loosely into polythene bags and stand them level inside the freezer until they are solidly frozen. Expel all air from the bag, seal and label as to contents. Cooked tarts, which may be accidentally squashed, should be wrapped gently in foil and stored in rigid plastic containers.

Freezer Life. According to the filling, usually 4–6 months.

To Use. Cook raw tarts direct from the freezer at an oven temperature appropriate to the type of pastry. Leave cooked tarts to thaw at room temperature for several hours before serving.

Game

Preparation. Game birds *must* be hung before freezing. After hanging, remove head, feet and accessible pellets. Pluck and draw the bird, wiping the carcass inside and out. Game is best frozen raw and unstuffed, but game cooked before freezing should be casseroled to prevent flesh drying.

Freezing. Pack raw birds separately in strong polythene bags and seal tightly. Cooked game dishes should be frozen in containers with HEADSPACE.

Freezer Life. Up to 2 months for uncooked birds and prepared dishes.

To Use. Thaw uncooked birds in closed bag at room temperature overnight. Older birds can then be marinaded. Reheat prepared dishes in tightly-lidded cooking pots in a slow oven, basting regularly as soon as the sauce is thawed.

Garlic

The flavour of garlic tends to weaken in reheated food, so those who enjoy a strong aroma may wish to increase slightly the quantity used in any recipe taken from a cookery book. The flavour will be retained more fully if the crushed cloves are put into the pan when olive oil is used for cooking, and left while the oil heats to cooking temperature. Care should be taken that the crushed pieces do not cook too fast and turn brown.

Glass

Glass jars, dishes or bowls must never be used as freezer containers. Oven-glass pie dishes or casseroles, provided they are guaranteed to withstand extremes of temperature, can be used to hold foil-wrapped food until it has frozen. Untoughened glass, jam jars or even preserving jars, may

111

splinter dangerously on being taken out of the freezer. For safety's sake, *any* oven-glass dish should have an interval at room temperature before being put into the oven.

Goose

The rich, fatty meat on a goose is not ideal freezer material, except in the very short-term. Dishes containing pieces of goose should be deemed to have a freezer-life dictated by this one ingredient—no more than 4–6 weeks. Uncooked geese are prepared and frozen as CHICKEN, which see.

Gooseberries

Preparation. Top and tail large, ripe (but not over-ripe) gooseberries. Pick over the fruit, discarding any with bruised or broken skin. Wash the berries in a colander or wire basket under running cold water, carefully shake dry. Gooseberries *can* be frozen dry—without sugar or syrup—but they are among the few summer fruits which are improved by sugaring before freezing. Two methods are effective—put the fruit in a deep dish, layer by layer, with 4 oz. of castor sugar to every pound of fruit. Leave until the fruit begins to soften and dissolve the sugar. Or a 30% SYRUP can be made and left to become quite cold before putting in the fruit.

Freezing. 'Dry' gooseberries are frozen in polythene bags. Keep the bags flat for convenient storage. As much air as possible should be pressed out of the bag by smoothing the surface from the bottom upwards, and the bag tied firmly at the neck with a plastic-covered wire tie. Sugared fruit can be packed in polythene bags, placed in sugar cartons. HEAD-SPACE must be left at the top of the bag between fruit and tie. Sugar syrup is poured into plastic or waxed containers to the half-way mark and the fruit pressed down into it. Crumpled greaseproof or polythene is placed on top of the fruit to keep it submerged beneath the syrup. Leave HEADSPACE and seal.

Freezer Life. Up to 1 year.

To Use. Leave the fruit in bags or containers in the refrigerator overnight if it is to be served cold with cream. If it is to be cooked, use directly from the freezer.

Gougères

Preparation. See also CHOUX PASTRY. Make pastry according to chosen recipe, beating in 2 or 3 tablespoons of grated Parmesan or Cheddar cheese with the eggs. Put the pastry by tablespoonfuls on a baking sheet, hollowing the centres with the back of a spoon, or spread it evenly round an oiled foil pie dish. Cut circles of non-stick baking paper, and place these lightly into the centre of the pastry. Cook according to recipe, and most carefully take out the paper when the pastry is cooling—do not pull or tear the crisply cooked pastry case.

Freezing. Put the small gougère cases side by side in a plastic box in layers, with foil between the layers. Put a large case alone in a box, seal and label adding 'with care'.

Freezer Life. Up to 6 months.

To Use. Prepare a richly-flavoured filling of chicken livers or chicken, veal and/or ham, cooked with TOMATO PURÉE, STOCK or WHITE SAUCE. Fill the gougères and reheat for only a few minutes in a brisk oven.

Green peas

Preparation. Do not freeze peas bought from a town green-grocer. Garden-grown peas should be picked when the shells are bright green and crisp. Shell the peas, check for and discard wormy specimens. BLANCH for $1\frac{1}{2}$ minutes.

Freezing. Pack the peas loosely in polythene bags. Freeze until they are individually frozen and can be shaken down and packed more compactly. Seal the bags with plastic-covered wire ties.

Freezer Life. Up to 1 year.

To Use. Put the frozen peas straight from the freezer into the minimum boiling water for up to 5 minutes, drain and put back in the pan with a knob of butter. Peas can also be cooked with butter and with care on a bed of lettuce leaves in a closely-lidded pan. Guard against overcooking, in either case.

Ham

Ham, and dishes containing ham in slices or cubes, should be stored in a freezer for a short time only. The high salt content of the cured meat makes it turn rancid in a short space of time. It will not be 'bad', but will have a peculiar taste. Any prepared dish containing ham can be kept for about 6–8 weeks in the freezer. It is usually possible to include the ham when the dish is being reheated for serving, if longer storage is required. Ham joints will be satisfactory for up to 2 months.

Hare

Preparation. Behead and bleed hare as soon as possible after killing, leaving to hang in a cool place for up to 24 hours. Skin and draw the hare, wash and dry. Cut it into joints if these will be required for the subsequent cooking. Shop-bought hares will usually be already prepared, and can be jointed or frozen whole.

Freezing. Wrap the whole or jointed hare very securely in a thick polythene bag, pressing the polythene closely down with the flat of the hand to exclude air pockets and sealing with a plastic-covered wire tie.

Freezer Life. 4–6 months for freshly-shot hare, 2–3 for shop bought.

To Use. Thaw a whole hare for 24 hours at room temperature before cooking, joints for 3–4 hours.

Haricots verts

Preparation. These delicious beans are seldom to be found in greengrocers' shops, but should be grown wherever possible. Pick when the pods are dark green, but not more than three or four inches long. Wash, top and tail and BLANCH for 3 minutes.

Freezing. Loosely pack the whole beans in polythene bags, freeze and pack more compactly when individual beans are frozen solid.

Freezer Life. Up to 1 year.

To Use. Cook the beans straight from the freezer in boiling water for 1 minute. Drain, return to the pan with a little water, butter, pepper and salt and heat, shaking the pan occasionally.

Headspace

A term used to describe the space left at the top of containers when liquid or semi-solid food is poured in. This space is essential, because it allows room for expansion during freezing without pushing the lid off the container or breaking out of a waxed carton. Headspace is left in polythene bags by tying the neck of the bag an inch or so above the level of the food inside. Usually $\frac{1}{2}$ inch in wide containers and 1 inch in tall narrow containers is sufficient headspace to leave.

Heat, sources of

Although a home freezer will operate successfully if it is placed in close proximity to a source of heat—e.g., cooker, boiler, washing machine or radiator—the motor may cut in and out at shorter than usual intervals, thus increasing the running costs. With this proviso, lack of a cool position is no deterrent to choosing a freezer. See also POSITIONING OF A FREEZER.

Herbs

Fresh or home-frozen herbs are inevitably superior to dried herbs bought by the packet, and should be used wherever possible in freezer cooking. Dried oregano should never be used in food cooked for the freezer—it develops a thoroughly objectionable flavour. Packeted thyme is not much better. If fresh herbs are unobtainable, and cannot be grown even in pots on a window sill, the only truly acceptable substitutes are the imported French variety, packed in sprigs in polythene bags. The following collection of herbs is suggested to cover freezer cooking requirements.

Balm. Buy a single root, which will form an adequate and long-lasting bush. Chop the leaves, freeze, use in making apple jelly, cooking with hard fruit particularly pears.

Basil. Must be planted in seed boxes in warmth before being planted out in early summer. It dislikes draughty or damp situations. Freeze and use for flavouring all tomato dishes, or pasta, or vegetable soup.

Bay. A green bay tree counts as ordinary garden foliage, or as a potted tree, but the fresh leaves have a different and finer flavour than dried leaves.

Chives. Buy in a clump, divide as it expands, replace after two or three seasons. Cut chives with sharp scissors, chop with scissors or a knife, not in a blender. Freeze for use with salads, tomato or egg dishes, or in salad dressing.

Fennel. A very large, feathery plant that never quite justifies the amount of space it demands. The flavour is very strong. A little can be frozen for using with fish.

Garlic. Put a dozen cloves of garlic in a saucer of water in early spring, and leave until roots begin to develop. Plant in the sunniest possible place, and if the summer is hot a crop of garlic can be picked and dried in early autumn. Garlic will fail completely in a chilly damp summer, but nothing is lost in trying. Tie the green shoots together in a bunch and hang the bulbs up in an airy place to dry for use throughout the winter.

Marjoram. An annual plant to be used on its own account, or in place of oregano. Plant a whole packet of seeds and use the seedlings, rather than thinning out. Freeze and mix with thyme and savory for 'mixed herbs' where required. Use with lamb, or with vegetables cooked in butter, or in soup or occasionally as a variant in salad dressing.

Mint. Apple mint, with soft, broad green leaves is preferable to the narrow-leafed spearmint. Plant a single root with fencing round it below soil level, or it will smother neighbouring plants. Pull out all stems that remain in autumn. Freeze for making mint sauce, with stuffing or topping for lamb, or mint jelly with apples, and occasionally in savoury stuffing.

Parsley. Buy seeds rather than roots. Cover the seeds with hot water for a few minutes before planting, to speed germination. Sow twice during the year. Strong plants may last for 2 seasons, but annual planting is recommended. Either freeze sprigs whole or chop leaves and freeze, in individual plastic/polythene jam-pots or polythene bags. Use stems for BOUQUETS GARNIS.

Sage. Choose short, sturdy roots, not those with woody, straggling stems. Plant deeply and it will make a large bush, lasting for many years. Chop and freeze the leaves, use for stuffing, in pork dishes, game, or as extra seasoning for boiled suet puddings or the pastry for raised pies. Use sage sparingly in cooking for the freezer as its flavour tends to increase during frozen storage.

Savory. The perennial winter savory is most widely used for home growing, but an annual variety is obtainable. Freeze and use for flavouring vegetable dishes, beans particularly, or in emergency use where marjoram is called for.

Tarragon. Buy roots of French tarragon, one or two only, for it is prolific. Mark its place in the earth in winter, because it disappears completely. Chop the leaves, freeze, use with chicken, fish and egg dishes.

Thyme. One sturdy root will last almost a lifetime. Cut back well when taking the leaves for freezing. Chop finely, freeze and use sparingly for all savoury stuffings, for salad dressings, tomato dishes, pasta, soup. Use in BOUQUETS GARNIS.

Hollandaise sauce

This sauce is basically an emulsion with a basis of butter, egg yolks and lemon juice or vinegar. It should not be attempted for home freezing. The sauce can be prepared commercially with the use of stabilizers to prevent separation on freezing and thawing but these are not available to the public.

Home freezer

An appliance designed to freeze a given weight of food within 24 hours as well as being suitable to store commercially quick-frozen foods. Some home freezers can achieve an internal air temperature as low as −29°C. (−20°F.) The lowest possible temperature should be employed to freeze food, but, once frozen it is most economical to store food at −18°C. (0°F.) Lower temperatures of storage will increase the running cost of a freezer without bringing a significant increase in storage life.

Home removal

When moving house, the distance to be travelled and the time it will take are the deciding factors *vis à vis* the freezer. If the journey is a long one, taking more than a few hours door to door, the freezer will have to be emptied, cleaned and re-filled from scratch at the new home. If a journey of less than a few hours is involved, a fully-packed freezer wrapped securely round with several layers of rugs and/or sacking, will travel without the contents thawing. It should be the last object to be unplugged before the electricity is cut off, the last to be loaded on to the furniture van and the first to be unloaded and immediately plugged in to the mains. Make sure that the removal men understand the weight of the loaded freezer, and check with the INSURANCE company that the freezer will be covered for travelling under an existing policy.

Ice cubes

A large supply of ice cubes can conveniently be kept in the freezer. If the plastic dividing compartments of a refrigerator tray can be spared, the cubes should be turned out of the tray and packed in the divider—if turned loosely into a poly-thene bag, they will freeze into an awkward mass. The small plastic globes filled with water can more easily be kept in the freezer for using with iced drinks.

Ice-cream

Commercially-made ice-cream is obtainable at a great financial saving in half-gallon cans from any reputable firm or bulk-purchase supplier of frozen food. The can, or bricks of ice-cream, should be stored well down in the coolest part of a chest-type home freezer, or firmly against the cooling coils of an upright freezer. Take out serving quantities with a scoop, or a tablespoon with a strong handle that will not bend under pressure, and return the can to the freezer without delay. Home-made ice-cream does not have to be stirred during freezing in a home freezer. The freezing process is too rapid to allow large crystals to form in the mixture, as happens in the frozen food compartment of a domestic refrigerator.

Icing

See CAKE ICING.

Insulation

A home freezer is insulated by expanded plastic foam, pumped between the inner and outer walls of the cabinet and the door. Care is taken to ensure a good seal of joints in the casing. Cooling tubes convey refrigerant around the freezer and the insulation inhibits entry of heat from the outside air.

Insurance

A vital precaution for the freezer owner, an insurance policy to cover loss of contents from most causes will cost from about £2 per annum for every £75 worth of stored food. Electricity showrooms, dealers and bulk suppliers will advise on

117

insurance. A policy is usually conditional upon a maintenance contract being taken out with an approved refrigeration engineer, at a cost of about £5 per annum. The contract will cover a 24-hour service in case of breakdown, and an annual servicing and inspection of the freezer mechanism.

Jam fruit

To save the heat and effort of making jam in summer weather, fruit for jam-making can be picked over and put into the freezer in polythene bags without any ceremony. At any convenient later stage, the frozen fruit is put straight into a preserving pan on the stove and heated gently until thawing is complete. The juice will then run more readily and the boiling time is not extended.

Jam tarts

Uncooked jam tarts, fully assembled, are not good freezer material as the jam never freezes and is permanently sticky. It is better to use pastry from the freezer and make up jam tarts as they are required.

Kale

Preparation. Although little known, kale may be frozen successfully. Winter kale is at its best in a short season during December and January. Only home- or garden-grown produce should be frozen. Pick the leaves when they are crisp and tender, cut off any stalk and pull out any strings in the 'rib' down the centre of the leaf. Wash and BLANCH for 4 minutes.

Freezing. Make up bundles of serving quantities, put in polythene bags, fold the bag round the bundle, seal and label.

Freezer Life. Up to 1 year.

To Use. Put the kale directly from the freezer into boiling salted water and cook for no more than 7–10 minutes. Serve with melted butter.

Kebabs

Preparation. Cubes of lamb cut from the top of the leg or cubes of rump steak can be used for kebabs. If pork is used freezer life is reduced accordingly. Marinade the meat for a few hours in a mixture of red or white wine, olive oil, crushed garlic and herbs to taste. A little ground black pepper and a very little salt may be added. Thread the cubes of meat on to the skewers of a kebab fitment, or on to wooden skewers— not on to butcher's metal skewers which are not of stainless metal—alternately with small onions or slices of onion cut downwards from top to root, mushrooms, and squares of green pepper. Freeze before cooking. If time is short, the marinaded meat can be frozen by itself, but time will have to be allowed for thawing before skewering for cooking. Freeze the marinade separately.

Freezing. Pad the sharp ends of the filled skewers with foil or kitchen paper or with small corks if available. Wrap each skewer separately in foil, turning over the ends of the foil to make a secure parcel. Overwrap several skewers in a strong polythene bag, seal and label. Freeze the marinade separately, label. If marinaded meat is to be frozen without skewering, put the cubes of meat very close together in straight lines in a foil baking dish or tray, cover with marinade and with a piece of foil and overwrap. Seal tightly and label.

Freezer Life. 3–4 months for lamb, 2 months for pork.

To Use. Add a small tomato to each skewer and cook skewered kebabs directly from the freezer. Thaw the marinading liquor at room temperature for a few hours, and use as basting liquid. Unskewered meat should be thawed in the refrigerator overnight, but not left at room temperature before cooking.

Kidneys

Preparation. Kidneys bought ready-frozen should be put straight into the home-freezer after purchase, not allowed to become even partly thawed if they are not to be used immediately. Kidneys prepared in sauce should be only *just* cooked before freezing. Any cream should be left out at first cooking, and wine used according to freezer practice. (See WINE.) If not purchased frozen, raw kidneys should be prepared in the usual way by skinning, removing the core and excess fat, washing and drying.

Freezing. Interleave kidneys with double polythene and overwrap in a polythene bag. Put cooled, cooked kidney into plastic or waxed containers, or in a foil-lined ovenproof dish. Remove the foil package when contents are solid. Overwrap foil package in polythene bag. Seal and label.

Freezer Life. 3–4 months.

To Use. Turn cooked kidneys out of containers, or take foil packages out of polythene bags, and reheat the food in lidded serving dishes set over a pan of simmering water. If reheating must be done in the oven, keep the dishes closely covered to avoid drying out. If necessary, blend in a few spoonfuls of extra STOCK, or some TOMATO PURÉE if this is included in the recipe. Add any required cream, wine or bacon snippets, previously cooked, when thawing is complete. Thaw uncooked kidney and cook in any way desired.

Kitchen foil	An indispensable material for packing food for the freezer, because it can be wrapped firmly round meat, poultry or fish to make an air-tight and well-protected parcel. Foil can also be used to line earthenware or oven-proof dishes before filling them with cooked food for freezing. A large margin of foil should be left outside the dish and the lid set in place until the contents are solid. The margin is then folded over and pressed closely on to the frozen food, the package being taken out of the dish and overwrapped in a polythene bag and sealed. Foil should only be used for overwrapping meat or poultry if the bones are first wrapped with polythene, etc. For freezer purposes, the heavy-gauge foil should be chosen.
Kohlrabi	*Preparation.* Only home or garden-grown kohlrabi should be considered for freezing. Pick when small, young and tender. Trim off green, wash and peel thinly. Very small specimens may be left whole, others cut into wedges and BLANCHED for 3 minutes. *Freezing.* Pack the kohlrabi into polythene bags, tie loosely and freeze on wire trays until firm. When the vegetable is firm, separate the wedges by gently shaking or pressing the bag, seal and label. If serving quantities can be accurately gauged, pack closely into plastic or waxed boxes. *Freezer Life.* Up to 1 year. *To Use.* Cook kohlrabi directly from the freezer, in a small quantity of fast boiling water, for 5–7 minutes.
Labelling	All food intended for storage in the freezer should be labelled with the contents of the package, the weight of the food, and the date of freezing. Food with a limited freezer-life should be dated, and the date noted on the FREEZER LIST, which see. Specially prepared freezer labels can be bought, some ordinary sticky labels will serve. Some, however, do not remain in position during storage—suitable types can only be found by trial and error. The label will be secure if it is marked on the sticky side with a laundry marking or felt-tip pen, and stuck to the inside of the bag. Plastic or waxed boxes can be marked directly with a chinagraph or Pentel, or with a stick-on label over-stuck with freezer tape to prevent it peeling off in the freezer.
Labels	Gummed labels specially treated to remain in place under freezer conditions can be bought in sheets from leading

stationers or directly from the suppliers of freezer containers—
they are not essential. Luggage labels tied on to the package
or secured to the wire tie of polythene bags will be adequate.
Also see LABELLING.

Lamb

Lamb is a good freezer subject, cooked or raw. The fatty
breast of lamb is the only cut that should not, ideally, be
frozen, and certainly not for any length of time. See also
MEAT—PURCHASE OF, FREEZING, PACKING. Also
CHOPS, MOUSSAKA, KEBABS.

Freezer Life. Up to 9 months for raw lean lamb.

Lasagne

Preparation. Boil the squares of lasagne in a large pan containing the maximum quantity of salted water. Cook until
they are tender, but not floppy and discoloured. Prepare or
thaw a quantity of RAGU, or cooked minced beef, and an
equal volume of WHITE SAUCE. Add a good scraping of
nutmeg to the sauce during preparation or reheating.
Grease foil-lined ovenproof dishes, square cake tins or foil
baking dishes with a trace of vegetable oil. Put a layer of
ragu, or cooked minced beef, on the bottom of the dishes,
then a layer of white sauce, and cover with squares of
lasagne. Continue in this way until the dishes are filled to
within an inch of the top, ending with a layer of lasagne
covered by another of white sauce. Already frozen ragu, or
cooked minced beef, should not ideally be used for making
lasagne which is itself to be frozen. The second cooking may
dry it out and spoil the flavour. Frozen ragu, or cooked
minced beef, can be used, however, if the dish is to be eaten
immediately.

Freezing. Keep level inside the freezer until the food is
solidly frozen. Then remove the foil package from the ovenproof dish if this is used. Cover closely with foil and overwrap
in a polythene bag. Seal and label.

Freezer Life. 2–3 months.

To Use. Replace foil package in ovenproof dish or uncover
foil dishes, sprinkle a lavish amount of grated parmesan
cheese on top of the frozen sauces, and cook for at least an
hour in a moderate oven. If the lasagne seems to be drying, or
the edges crisping too much before the centre is cooked,
cover loosely with a piece of foil and reduce the heat.

Lettuce

Lettuce will not freeze and thaw satisfactorily. The leaves
have a high water-content and would be limp, khaki-
coloured and uneatable.

121

Liver

Preparation. Liver should not be cooked and frozen in large pieces because the texture tends to become leathery on reheating. However, if covered completely with sauce or gravy cooked liver will probably be satisfactory for a few weeks. If frozen raw, cut into slices first. Chicken livers should be carefully picked over, and all greenish marks from the bile sac scraped off.

Freezing. Freeze slices of raw liver in polythene bags, with double pieces of foil between successive slices. Chicken livers should be wrapped in foil, overwrapped in a polythene bag, sealed and labelled.

Freezer Life. Up to 2 months.

To Use. Separate slices of liver as soon as they have begun to soften, and cook in the usual way. Allow chicken livers to soften before sautéeing in butter to make PÂTÉ or using in RAGU, which see, or in stuffing. Reheat cooked liver covered in a slow oven, guarding against drying.

Loganberries

As RASPBERRIES.

Macaroni cheese

It is not worth making up this dish completely before freezing as it takes such a long time to heat through. However, macaroni cheese can be prepared in a matter of minutes from frozen white sauce and frozen grated cheese. For 4 portions boil 6 oz. quick-cooking macaroni until just tender, drain. Turn 1 pint of sauce into saucepan and heat gently until hot. Place layers of macaroni, white sauce and grated cheese in an ovenproof dish, sprinkle with more cheese and grill to a golden brown colour.

Mange-tout

Preparation. This rare variety of green pea is eaten whole, including the delicate pod. It is rarely, if ever, seen in shops, and shop-bought specimens would not be suitable for freezing in any case. They are not difficult to grow in any garden. Picked when very small, but with the peas formed within the pod, they are BLANCHED for 1 minute before freezing.

Freezing. In polythene bags, loosely packed and sealed. When frozen, pack closely and seal.

Freezer Life. Up to 1 year.

To Use. Simmer in a little water and a lot of butter for about 15 minutes, or until just tender.

Margarine

This is preferable to butter in cooking for the freezer, especially in sauces. Both butter and margarine are emulsions and that of margarine is more consistently stable during freezing

122

and thawing. Butter may, sometimes, tend to separate when incorporated into foods for the freezer.

Marrow

Preparation. Large marrow is only worth freezing in households where it is a great favourite. Cut the marrow into rings, peel and take out seeds. Steam gently until tender, drain thoroughly, then mash with salt and freshly ground black pepper. Cool before freezing. See also COURGETTES.

Freezing. Put the mashed marrow in serving quantities in plastic or waxed containers, leaving HEADSPACE.

Freezer Life. About 6 months.

To Use. Turn the frozen marrow out of its container into a bowl set over a pan of simmering water or into a thick saucepan. Cover closely, heat until thawed and very hot, drain again and adjust seasoning.

Mayonnaise

Home-made mayonnaise will not freeze satisfactorily. The mixture separates irretrievably, and cannot be beaten back into an acceptable emulsion. Experts can produce a freezable mayonnaise by using stabilizers, but these are not generally available.

Meat, butchering of

Butchering meat is a skilled job, and not one to be undertaken lightly in the preparation of meat for home freezing. Unskilled butchering leads to ragged joints and cuts, which are wasteful in carving. If fresh, unfrozen meat is bought in bulk from a retail butcher, he should be asked to prepare the carcass, and he must be expected to charge for this service. For freezing, excess fat should be trimmed off during butchering, the skin of pork scored to a quarter-inch depth, but the skin should not be taken off loins of lamb. Remember that a jointed side or half side of an animal will take several days to freeze as only one tenth the total freezer capacity should be used in any 24-hour period. The meat waiting to be frozen should be kept in the refrigerator or you could ask the butcher to store it for you in the chill cabinet. See MEAT, FREEZING OF.

Meat, freezing of

All meat must be frozen as rapidly as possible, to retain the good texture and flavour. Put the securely wrapped parcels of meat in the coldest part of the freezer. If possible, avoid opening the freezer at all while meat is freezing. Do not attempt to exceed the rule of freezing only one tenth by weight of the freezer's total capacity in any 24 hours. Frozen meat should be given ample time to thaw right through before being cooked. CHOPS and STEAKS are exceptions. A very large joint should be left in its freezer wrapping in the refrigerator for 24 hours, small joints overnight. If thawing positively must be hurried, stand the wrapped meat in a bowl and leave the cold water tap running over it for as long as possible.

Meat—leftovers

Preparation. Leftover portions of meat can be frozen for later use. It is most important that leftovers should be frozen as soon as possible after the original cooking. On no account must they be left uncovered at room temperature, or even for very long in the refrigerator. See also REFREEZING. Leftovers of roasted meat are best considered for use in stews or casseroles, and frozen in cubes with any remaining gravy. Meat cooked in sauce should be entirely covered with its remaining sauce. Slices of meat may become very dry during storage if packed without sauce or gravy.

Freezing. Put the meat, with sauce or gravy, in a shallow foil tray or foil baking dish, keeping it immersed in the liquid. Cover the dish with a piece of foil leaving HEADSPACE, overwrap in a polythene bag, seal and label.

Freezer Life. Up to 2 months.

To Use. Reheat in a moderate oven, directly from the freezer, leaving the foil covering on the dish throughout. Serve immediately.

Meat, packing of

Joints of meat should have all projections—ribs, bones, shanks—wrapped with folded greaseproof or kitchen paper, before putting into strong, gusseted polythene bags. The polythene is pressed firmly down on to the meat, using the flat of the hand to expel all air pockets and tied with a plastic-coated wire tie. Very large joints—legs of lamb, pork or veal, saddles of lamb, H-bones or ribs of beef—should, ideally, be wrapped firmly in a sheet of polythene and sealed with sticky tape before overwrapping in a bag. It is particularly important that the surface of meat should not be exposed to air inside the freezer, and secure packaging will prevent this. See individual entries for CHOPS and STEAKS.

Meat pies

Preparation. Pork, veal or mutton pies which are to be eaten as a cold meal are made and frozen in individual foil dishes rather than in large-size pie dishes. The meat content is usually very dense, and a large pie would take too long to thaw. No hard-boiled eggs should be included in pies for the freezer. Meat pies are made and cooked in the usual way,

124

with the meat finely cut up and put inside a case of hot-water crust, and the bones and trimmings simmered to a jelly to fill the cold pie. For freezer purposes, the meat should be a little more highly seasoned than would seem reasonable if the pie were to be eaten at once—a chopped leaf or two of sage can be put in with pork, marjoram with veal and rosemary with mutton, all helping to bring out the flavour of the meat.

Shop-bought cooked meat pies, except quick-frozen, should not be stored in a home freezer.

Steak and kidney pie, to be eaten hot as a main meal, can be prepared in a large pie dish—the meat being previously cooked and the raw pastry set on top over a pie funnel.

Freezing. Freeze small meat pies without added stock, but freeze the stock in a separate, labelled container. Put the pies in the freezer in plastic containers, or in polythene bags if they can stand alone on a level surface inside the freezer until the meat has frozen and the pastry is hard enough to withstand storage without being damaged. Steak and kidney pies should be covered with foil and overwrapped in a large plastic bag. Stand the dish level in the freezer until the meat and gravy are frozen.

Freezer Life. 4–5 months. The meat, not the pastry, determines the freezer life.

To Use. Put small pies into the refrigerator overnight, together with the relevant containers of frozen stock.

Three or four hours before serving, check that the stock has thawed to the point where it will pour into the pies through the usual hole in the top. If it remains half-thawed, stir it well with a fork to make it sufficiently liquid to pour. Fill the pies with stock, which will jel again after contact with the still-cold meat filling. Thereafter leave at room temperature until serving time. Steak and kidney pies can be cooked directly from the freezer. Cook at a high temperature to raise the pastry, and the meat will be thawed and heated during the cooking time, which will be slightly extended. If the pie is very large, the pastry may be ready before the meat is properly thawed. In this case, cover the pastry with a dampened sheet of greaseproof paper, lower the heat and leave the pie in the oven until the meat *is* ready.

Meat, purchase of   Bulk purchase of meat depends upon budget, freezer capacity and the reliability of the butcher. The capital outlay on a quarter-side of beef, half a pig or a whole carcass of veal or lamb is very great—56 lb. of beef will cost upwards of

125

£15—and it must be considered that cheap *and* expensive cuts are included in the overall price per pound. If shin of beef, brisket, breast of lamb or belly pork are seldom bought or used, the economy will largely be lost, or at least only maintained under duress. Bulk meat should not be bought without being tested for quality by freezing, cooking and eating. Private firms offering bulk supplies of frozen food will usually offer meat frozen and packed ready for the home freezer, but a sample should always be taken first. Such firms will also offer packs of selected cuts prepared for the freezer, but the price will be higher than if a whole carcass or portion of a beast were bought.

Meat uses a great deal of freezer space during storage, because few cuts will pack into the desirable rectangular shape.

In general, bulk purchase of meat is not the best idea if freezer space is restricted. But bought for a large freezer, on favourable terms, top-quality home-frozen meat will prove very convenient.

Meat sauce

Preparation. Meat sauce, for serving with pasta or as pancake or pasty filling, can be prepared for the freezer in multiples of the basic 2 pint quantity: 1 lb. minced beef, 1 large onion, 1 carrot, 2 sticks of celery, 4 oz. mushrooms—fresh or frozen, one glass of red wine, 1 tablespoon TOMATO PURÉE, $\frac{3}{8}$ pint of STOCK, fresh or frozen marjoram or basil, 1–2 oz. flour, salt and pepper. Cook the onion in two tablespoons of olive oil until golden brown. Chop the vegetables and mushrooms and stir for a few minutes with the oil and onion. Add the meat and stir it round thoroughly until the surfaces are browned. Sprinkle flour over the meat and stir in. Add the wine and purée, herbs and seasoning. Cook all together for a few minutes, then pour on the stock by degrees—the sauce should not be too moist. Continue to cook for about 15 minutes, with the lid partly covering the pan until the sauce is thick and rich-smelling. Cool in a bowl set in cold water.

Freezing. Put the sauce in serving quantities in plastic or waxed containers—margarine cartons are suitable—leaving HEADSPACE. Seal and label.

Freezer Life. 4–5 months.

To Use. Turn the sauce into a thick pan, set on low heat and leave covered until quite thawed. Stir to break up any remaining frozen areas, add more stock if necessary. When the sauce is hot, stir in some additional wine. Adjust seasoning before serving.

Melon

Cubes of slightly under-ripe melon can be frozen in a 30% sugar syrup as a meal starter. Small pieces of stem ginger give a good flavour. See SYRUP.
Freezer Life. Up to 6 months.

Meringues

Preparation. Hard meringues for freezing are made in the usual way, with egg whites and castor sugar, and can be frozen as shells ready for filling with cream or as elaborate cases for fruit or ice-cream. Although meringues will keep *fairly* well in a sealed tin outside the freezer, they will keep *beautifully* in the freezer.
Freezing. Put meringues in a plastic box, label, and do not allow the box to lie under any heavy article, such as a joint of meat or a chicken. In an emergency, meringues can be frozen in a polythene bag, as long as they can remain on top of all other freezer contents.
Freezer Life. Up to 1 year.
To Use. Fill and decorate meringues direct from the freezer.

Soft meringues. A made-up pudding like Queen of Puddings with soft meringue topping can be prepared and kept in the freezer. The entire dish should be placed on the lid of a large tin and covered with the tin. Label base of tin 'this way up'.
To Use. Allow pudding to thaw at room temperature for about 2–3 hours and flash the meringue in a hot oven for a few minutes.

Milk

Whole milk, as bought from a dairy, cannot usually be frozen successfully, because the fat will separate. Homogenized milk can be frozen for use in emergency, but should not be stored for longer than three months. It should be stored in a waxed carton or plastic bottle, allowing HEADSPACE, and thawed in the refrigerator.

Mince pies

Mince pies can be made 4–6 weeks before Christmas. If one large mince pie is made in preference to several small ones, it should be frozen on a foil pie plate and kept in a plastic box before cooking. As with the small pies, leave at room temperature for about half an hour before cooking in a hot oven. When the pastry is well risen and brown, check that the thick filling of mincemeat is also properly thawed and hot. If extra time is needed, cover the pie with a piece of greaseproof paper.

127

Moussaka

Moussaka can be made with leftover lamb or beef. The meat should be minced and made up as soon as possible after its first cooking.

Preparation. About 1 lb. minced lamb or beef is required, 1 onion, 1 aubergine, ¾ lb. tomatoes, salt, pepper, oil for frying, ½ pint cheese sauce. Peel and slice the onion and fry gently until soft. Add to cooked minced beef or lamb together with salt and pepper. Slice aubergine and remove excess moisture. Fry in oil until cooked through and lightly browned. Cool. Peel and slice the tomatoes.

Freezing. Place the meat mixture in a foil-lined ovenproof casserole or a deep foil baking dish. Cover with a layer of aubergines then tomatoes. Pour cooled cheese sauce over the tomato. Cover and freeze.

Freezer Life. 4–6 months.

To Use. Sprinkle 1–2 oz. grated cheese on top of moussaka. Heat at 425°F. (Gas Mark 7) for about 1–1½ hours. Brown under the grill if necessary.

Mousse

Preparation. Sweet or savoury mousses can be prepared for the freezer according to any favoured recipe. A mousse of crab, lobster or salmon should be made with absolutely fresh and not previously frozen fish. Ham mousse *can* be frozen, but only as a convenience for a day or two before serving. A mousse of game may be made with cooked and refrozen leftover meat, *provided that the meat was frozen immediately after first serving*. A mousse made thus should be eaten at once and not frozen otherwise its flavour will not be good. Sweet mousses of fruit or chocolate or coffee should be frozen without their decorations. Freeze as soon as the mixtures are set.

Freezing. Most mousse mixtures are firm enough to be turned out of their moulds before freezing. Turn them on to the *lid* of an adequately sized plastic bowl, and fix the bowl itself over the top. Hold the upturned bowl firmly when placing it on a level surface inside the freezer, and avoid knocking during storage.

Freezer Life. According to the freezer life of chosen meat or fish. Sweet mousses can be kept for up to 2 months.

To Use. Leave the upside-down bowl in the refrigerator for several hours, putting it at room temperature and uncovering the mousse about two hours before serving. To avoid having to lift the mousse, trim the edges of the lid with lettuce or watercress for a savoury mousse, cream, grated chocolate, fruit segments or even a little icing for sweet. Decorate the mousse according to type, and serve on the camouflaged lid set on a larger plate or a cake board.

Mushroom sauce

Fresh mushrooms, sliced and sautéed in butter, or frozen MUSHROOMS, are added to frozen WHITE SAUCE. The ingredients should be at roughly the same temperature when they are put together. If mushroom sauce is to be prepared in its entirety before freezing, use small button mushrooms. The flat variety with their black gills will discolour the sauce.
Freezer Life. Up to 6 months.

Mushrooms

Field mushrooms should only be frozen if you are absolutely sure that no inedible specimen of fungus has been included by mistake. Also check them for 'livestock'.
Preparation. Wash, skin when necessary and dry. Slice the mushrooms, or leave the smallest button variety whole, sauté for a few minutes in margarine. A large quantity can be sliced and deep-fried for one minute in a chip pan of vegetable oil. Drain the mushrooms on kitchen paper, then put them in a bowl and stand the bowl in cold water to cool the contents.
Freezing. Put mushrooms carefully into rigid plastic or waxed containers, setting them in layers with foil or greaseproof paper between.
Freezer Life. 3–4 months.
To Use. The mushrooms can be fried or added to a prepared dish direct from the freezer and reheated. For omelettes, they should be thawed at room temperature for 1–2 hours or heated in a buttered dish set over a pan of hot water.

Mustard sauce

To the required quantity of VELOUTÉ SAUCE, add French mustard to taste. Stir the mustard into the sauce after the liaison has been blended in. Adjust seasoning before serving.

Nectarines

See PEACHES.

Non-freezers

Specifically, foods which should not be frozen are very fat meat, hard-boiled eggs, lettuce, cucumbers, bananas, radishes, single cream, whole milk, table jellies, cornflour-based sauces and custards, egg custards and yoghurt. Spring onions, raw celery, and large tomatoes are suitable only for use in cooking after freezing.
Individually non-freezers are foods which nobody likes. These should not be bought and frozen, no matter how low the price.
Short-term freezers are bacon, ham and butter.

129

Onion sauce	*Preparation*. Add about 1 lb. boiled chopped onions to 1 pint of already frozen WHITE SAUCE. Onion sauce can be made for the freezer in its entirety, but the boiled onions should be very thoroughly drained before mixing with the waiting white sauce. Season with salt and white pepper.

Freezing. Freeze the sauce in plastic or waxed containers, leaving HEADSPACE. Seal and label.

Freezer Life. 4–6 months.

To Use. Hold the containers under running hot water until the contents can be pushed out. Reheat the sauce in a pan, stirring continuously once thawing has begun, or set in a covered basin over a pan of simmering water. If the sauce has separated during storage, beat briskly with a wooden spoon before serving. If consistency seems too thick, add a little milk during reheating.

Oranges

Fruits which are readily obtainable all the year round, such as oranges, lemons, grapefruit, do not generally repay the effort of freezing and are not a good use of home-freezer space.

However, Seville oranges and tangerines which have a short season freeze well. Also a prepared grapefruit and orange cocktail frozen with 30% sugar SYRUP makes a refreshing start to a meal. Cut out segments, removing all trace of membrane and pith.

Oven-glass

It is possible to freeze food in oven-glass dishes, bowls and plates, but not particularly desirable. The glass is heavy and bulky, likely to crush any lighter packages inside the freezer and takes up more space than a polythene or plastic container. Some oven-glass is guaranteed for freezer-to-oven use, but the possibility remains that the glass may shatter in the oven if the temperature is slightly higher than it can withstand. If the contents of the dish will stand partial thawing before cooking, the oven-glass should stand at room temperature for at least thirty minutes before going into the oven. Taken all round, it is better practice to line oven-glass dishes with KITCHEN FOIL, which see, before filling with food for freezing, taking out the frozen package and overwrapping with polythene for storage. The foil package is put back into the dish for re-heating, and the foil taken out when the food has thawed sufficiently.

Overcooking

Food is hardly ever spoiled by freezing, unless prepared or packed without due care, but frozen food can be ruined by overcooking. Experience and knowledge of the cooker are

130

the only true guides to the timing of frozen food, but all dishes with sauce or gravy should be guarded against drying in the oven. Frozen vegetables bought in bulk should be cooked *exactly* according to the directions on the packet. Home-frozen vegetables should be timed for cooking from the moment the water in the pan comes back to the boil, and allowed about one-quarter of the cooking time for market-fresh ones. Pre-cooked food should be very slightly less than ready for serving when it goes into the freezer—i.e., root vegetables or pulses in a casserole or stew should still have a trace of resistance to the fork, meat only just cooked right through, sauce only beginning to be reduced. Reheating in a slow to moderate oven will complete the cooking to perfection, without the dish drying out or vegetables breaking up or meat turning ragged. Once the dish has thawed but not heated to serving point, watch it carefully for signs of drying and, if necessary, cover the surface of food with foil and lower the oven temperature. Do not keep reheated food waiting on a hot-plate before serving.

Packaging for the freezer	See WRAPPING, also POLYTHENE, KITCHEN FOIL, PLASTIC BOXES, WAXED CONTAINERS, also PACKING THE FREEZER, and SEALING.
Packing the freezer	All packages should be wiped dry before they are placed against the walls of the freezer or in a freezer basket. Damp packages stick tightly to the nearest surface and any adjacent packages, and have to be wrestled free by force. All packages or boxes of food must be placed in the coldest place close to the walls until the food inside is solidly frozen. No more than one-tenth of the freezer's total capacity should be used for freezing fresh food in any twenty-four hour period. Packages and boxes should not be stacked closely until the food is solidly frozen. Rectangular packages which stack inside the freezer make the best use of available space. See individual entries for food, also WRAPPING.
Pancakes	*Preparation.* Make pancake batter according to any favoured recipe, allowing to stand for half-an-hour before cooking. Use a 7-inch base omelette pan, with no more than 2 tablespoons of batter for each pancake—keep the pan moving from side to side while pouring the batter in and it will spread to exactly the right thinness. Put the cooked pancakes on a wire cake cooling tray until the whole batch has been cooked. Allow to cool for a few minutes only, then freeze.

Freezing. Layer the pancakes with pieces of non-stick baking paper or double greaseproof, wrap in foil and over-wrap in a polythene bag. Expel all air, seal and label.

Freezer Life. 2–3 months.

To Use. Remove pancakes from their freezer wrapping, separate and leave for a few minutes until they have softened. Spread with chosen filling, roll up and put into a buttered shallow dish, possibly with strained melted jam or a fruit sauce poured over. Reheat under a loose covering of foil for 10 or 15 minutes only.

Parsley sauce

To the required quantity of VELOUTÉ SAUCE, add finely chopped fresh or frozen parsley. To make a very superior form of this sauce, pick a large bunch of parsley, strip the leaves from the stalks to give about 2 oz. per pint of sauce, and put them into boiling salted water for about five minutes. Purée the boiled parsley in a blender or by rubbing through a nylon sieve, and add it to the sauce. Adjust seasoning before serving.

Freezer Life. Up to 6 months.

Partridge

See GAME.

Pasta

See individual entries for MACARONI, SPAGHETTI, RAVIOLI, LASAGNE, also RAGU, MEAT SAUCE, TOMATO PURÉE.

Pastry

Preparation. Flaky, puff and shortcrust pastry can be made by any favoured method, in large quantities for freezing. Prepared puff pastry, bought ready frozen, is usually preferable to home-made, being invariably successful. Cut prepared pastry into weighed-out slabs of 1 or 2 lb. each, or line into foil pie dishes and prick the surface all over with a fork. Do not freeze a large, undivided lump of pastry as it will take too long to thaw when required for use.

Freezing. Wrap each weighed-out piece in foil or in a polythene bag. Overwrap several pieces in one large bag, seal and label with type of pastry and weight. Freeze pastry-lined pie dishes unwrapped and separately in the freezer until quite frozen, then interlay with foil and pack carefully in a large polythene bag. Do not subject the bag to any pressure inside the freezer, or handle carelessly, or the pie shells will shatter. If this happens, thaw, re-roll the pieces and use again immediately.

Freezer Life. Up to 1 year for flaky or shortcrust made with margarine and shortening, only 3–4 months for home-made puff pastry made with butter.

To Use. Leave the required amount of pastry in the refrigerator for a few hours, or overnight, allowing to stand at room temperature for about 1 hour before rolling. Fill and cook lined pie cases direct from the freezer, at a temperature suitable for type of pastry.

Pâté

Preparation. Meat or liver pâtés and terrines have a limited freezer life because the usual recipes require a high proportion of ham and/or bacon. It is therefore not wise to prepare for the freezer more of either dish than will be required for consumption within 4 weeks. See PÂTÉ OF CHICKEN LIVERS, TERRINES.

Pâté of chicken livers

Preparation. To make sufficient pâté for six good helpings, the following proportions are adequate: 1 lb. chicken livers, not previously frozen, 6 oz. of butter, 1 tablespoon each of brandy and port, 2 large cloves of garlic, salt, ground black pepper, half a teaspoonful of chopped fresh or frozen thyme, a blade of mace. Scrape off any greenish marks on the liver caused by the bile sac. Melt 2 oz. of butter in a wide frying pan and cook the whole livers gently for about 7–10 minutes, guarding against overcooking. Put the cooked livers into a blender, add brandy to the cooking pan and let it bubble to evaporate the spirit. Pour the port into the pan and stir it round, scraping up all the juices. Add this mixture to the livers in the blender with the garlic, roughly chopped, and seasonings. Add the remaining 4 oz. of butter, well softened or in pieces. Blend to a very smooth paste, and sieve to remove any coarse pieces if a smoother pâté is preferred.

If a blender is not available, beat livers, juices, garlic and seasonings and butter, and pass all through a sieve.

Freezing. Spread the pâté smoothly into rectangular oven-glass or earthenware dishes, cut through the mass at irregular spaces, to allow a choice in serving portions. Place in the freezer until very firm but not solidly frozen. Do not pour butter over the top. Remove portions from the container and interleave with foil. Wrap all pieces closely in foil and over-wrap in a polythene bag. Seal and label.

Freezer Life. 4 weeks only.

To Use. Take the whole or serving portions out of the freezer and leave in the refrigerator overnight. Allow to stand, covered, at room temperature for 3–4 hours before serving. If pâté is used too soon after removal from the freezer, the flavour will not develop properly.

Peaches

Preparation. If possible taste peaches in the shop before buying for the freezer—those with a poor or pallid flavour should not be frozen. Skin the peaches by dropping them into a pan of boiling water for a count of ten, then pouring away the hot water and replacing it with cold. Slice directly into shallow plastic or waxed containers, with 30% sugar SYRUP. Cut the fruit in wedges round the stone and discard the stone. To prevent browning keep all fruit submerged by placing crushed greaseproof or cellophane paper just under the surface of the syrup.

Freezing. Seal the containers. Label.

Freezer Life. 8–10 months.

To Use. Leave the peaches in their containers at room temperature for 4–5 hours. If thawing must be hastened, stand containers in cool water. Turn into a flat dish and leave covered until serving.

Pears, cooking

Preparation. Large, hard cooking pears are not worth buying for freezing, but can be frozen if home grown or available without cost. Peel the pears, cut out core and seeds, and place in a pressure cooker in quarters with water, sugar, about 6–8 oz. per pint of water, and balm leaves.

Test for tenderness, in case a further cooking period is required. Cool the pears in their own juice before freezing.

Freezing. Put the pears in one-pint waxed containers, pour the cooking syrup over them, pushing a wooden skewer or spoon-handle gently down into the container to dispel all air bubbles. Push crushed greaseproof or cellophane paper beneath the surface of the liquid. Leave HEADSPACE, seal and label.

Freezer Life. Up to 1 year.

To Use. Reheat pears in their syrup in a thick pan over gentle heat, or in a covered dish in the oven. For serving cold, leave at room temperature for several hours.

Pears, dessert

Preparation. Pick pears at a perfect stage of ripeness. Peel, core and quarter the fruit. Put it in a wire basket and lower into a pan of 30% SYRUP, previously brought to the boil. Cook for $1\frac{1}{2}$ minutes only. Lift out the pears on a draining spoon and leave on a flat dish. Pour the syrup into a bowl, stand it in cold water with ice-cubes until quite cold.

Freezing. As PEARS, COOKING.
Freezer Life. Up to 1 year.
To Use. As PEARS, COOKING.

Pease pudding

Preparation. Cook two or three times the usual quantity of pease pudding, according to any favoured recipe. Do not add butter to the mixture before freezing. Divide into serving quantities.

Freezing. Put serving quantities of the pudding into foil pudding bowls, leaving HEADSPACE. Cover with foil, over-wrap in a polythene bag, seal and label.

Freezer Life. 3–4 months.

To Use. Put the pudding straight from the freezer into a steamer pan, or turn out of the bowl into a double boiler. It will look dry and crumbly, and the consistency is restored by setting a large piece of butter to melt on top of the bowl during reheating and beating it into the mixture before serving.

Peppercorns

Freshly-ground pepper is preferable to the packeted type for freezer cooking—its flavour is sharper and fresher. White or black peppercorns can be put whole into stock or soup which is to be strained, or ground into PÂTÉS or TERRINES. See also SEASONING.

Peppers

Preparation. Green peppers are better freezer subjects than those which have turned red. The peppers should be quite firm, crisp when cut, and have glossy skins. Wipe the skins with a damp cloth, dry, remove the stalks and cut the peppers into $\frac{1}{4}$-inch slices. Discard seeds and membrane. Do not blanch.

Freezing. Pack the sliced peppers in plastic or waxed containers in layers, separating every two layers with a piece of greaseproof paper. They can be frozen in polythene bags, if care is taken not to break or crush them during freezing. Seal the containers with lids or a plastic-covered wire tie, without HEADSPACE.

Freezer Life. Up to 1 year.

To Use. Use the peppers direct from the freezer for adding to or including in prepared dishes. Slices which are not allowed to thaw completely will be crisp enough to use as garnish or in salads.

Pheasants

See GAME.

K

Pigeons

Preparation. See GAME. Pigeons are best if marinaded in a well-flavoured French dressing for a few hours before cooking and freezing. The marinading is vital to tenderize the meat, but it should not be done after freezing and before cooking—to be effective the birds would have to stand for too long at room temperature before cooking. When the required number of birds have been marinaded, either split them down the back or leave them whole, and brown gently in a thick stewpan in a mixture of oil and butter, with some finely chopped onion. When the outside of the meat has turned colour, stir in flour in quantity appropriate to the number of birds to be cooked, cook for a few minutes, then add well-flavoured STOCK to just cover the birds. Cover and cook for about 15 minutes. Add mushrooms, very small carrots and chopped celery. Continue cooking in the oven or on a hot-plate until the pigeons are tender but not beginning to leave the bone. Take out the birds and vegetables and leave aside. Boil the stock rapidly until it has reduced by about one-third. Only now add salt and pepper to taste. Put birds and vegetables back in the pan, cover closely with the lid, and cool under running water. Cool thoroughly to room temperature before freezing.

Freezing. Put the birds in serving quantities in foil baking dishes, or foil-lined serving dishes with an extra covering of foil. Press the birds well down into the sauce and overwrap foil dishes in polythene bags, expel all air, seal and label. Freeze foil-lined dishes until the contents are solid, take out foil package, overwrap in polythene, seal and label.

Freezer Life. 4–6 months.

To Use. Reheat foil dishes direct from the freezer in a slow oven. Put foil packages back in ovenproof dish or casserole, reheat until the foil can be withdrawn. Cover the top of the thawing birds with TOMATO PURÉE, and stir this through the dish when all is hot. Do not allow the birds to dry or the sauce to reduce, but add extra stock or purée. Adjust seasoning before serving.

Pissaladière

Preparation. This aromatic onion tart takes a long time to prepare, and it is thus as easy to make three as one. The following proportions are for a single 8-inch tart, and can be multiplied as desired. For the dough: 5 oz. of plain flour, or strong bread flour, $1\frac{1}{2}$ oz. of butter or luxury margarine, 1 egg, $\frac{1}{2}$ oz. fresh yeast, half a teaspoon of salt, $\frac{1}{4}$ teaspoon of ground black pepper, just enough tepid water to cream the yeast. Rub the butter into the flour, add salt and pepper, mix and bind with beaten egg and creamed yeast. Knead the dough until it is elastic and comes away cleanly from the bowl and does not stick to the fingers.

Form dough into a ball, stand in a covered bowl in a warm place until it has nearly doubled in size, taking 1½–2 hours. Prepare the filling: Slice 1 lb. of onions finely, skin and slice 3 ripe tomatoes, crush 3 cloves of garlic. Cook the onions and garlic very slowly in oil in a covered pan, not allowing them to brown, but only to seethe themselves until soft and transparent. Put in the tomatoes, salt and pepper. Leave the pan uncovered, so that the water from the tomatoes can evaporate, and cook very gently until the mixture is pulpy and rich-smelling. Knead the dough a second time, then spread it evenly over a large foil pie plate pressing it well out over the rim. Spread the filling right across the top, leaving hardly any dough on view. Leave the pie in a warm place for about 20 minutes, then cook in a hot oven 425°F. (Gas Mark 7) for 15 minutes, then 350°F. (Gas Mark 4) for 30 minutes. Cool before freezing.

Freezing. Pissaladière baked in a foil plate can be packed in a polythene bag, air excluded by pressing the underside of the plate against the polythene without touching the top more than necessary. Seal and label.

Freezer Life. 3–4 months.

To Use. Place anchovy fillets in lines across the pie, lattice fashion, and stoned black olives so that one is enclosed in each square. Brush exposed dough edges with oil. Reheat in a slow oven, lightly covering the pie with foil or greaseproof paper. Reheating can be done direct from the freezer, in the foil dish. If pissaladière is to be eaten cold, it should be left in the refrigerator overnight in its freezer wrapping, the anchovies and olives added and the pie left covered at room temperature for 3 or 4 hours before serving.

Pizza

Preparation. The following quantities make three pizzas in 8-inch pie plates, and can be multiplied as required: 6 oz. of plain flour, or strong bread flour, ½ oz. of fresh yeast, a pinch of sugar, an egg, 2 oz. butter, ½ teaspoon of salt, ¼ teaspoon of black pepper, 1 tablespoon of grated Parmesan cheese, a little tepid water (about 3 fl. oz.). Dissolve the sugar in the water and add yeast to form a cream. Rub the fat into the flour with the salt, pepper and cheese, add beaten egg and creamed yeast mixture. If the dough is too dry, add a very little more tepid water. Beat the mixture until it is smooth, then knead on a floured board for 5–10 minutes. Put the ball of dough in a bowl, cover with a cloth and leave to stand in a warm place until the dough has doubled in volume. Knead again, divide into 3 pieces and press each piece into a foil plate. Cut 6 ripe skinned tomatoes into thick, horizontal slices and press the slices into the dough. Sprinkle with more Parmesan and plenty of fresh or frozen basil and/or marjoram.

Brush the pizzas all over with olive oil, cover and leave in a warm place for about thirty minutes, until the dough has risen again. Cook in a hot oven at 400°F. (Gas Mark 6) for 20–30 minutes. After cooking, cover the hot pizzas with a clean tea towel and leave on a cooling tray for 10 minutes. Allow them to become quite cold before freezing.

Freezing. Wrap the pizzas separately in polythene bags, seal. Three pizzas can then be overwrapped in a larger bag and frozen together.

Freezer Life. Up to 6 months.

To Use. Top the frozen pizzas with any combination of the following: mushrooms, fresh and partly-cooked, or frozen, sardines, slices of ham, anchovies, olives, sliced hard-boiled eggs covered with slices of Gruyère cheese, or rashers of thin streaky bacon. Reheat in a moderate oven, lightly covered with foil or a piece of greaseproof paper.

Plastic boxes

Rectangular boxes of rigid plastic, with tightly fitting lids, are obtainable in many sizes and can be used indefinitely as freezer containers, thus justifying the capital outlay. They do not usually need to be sealed at the edges with adhesive tape. Cheap or given-away-with-the-soap boxes are not often suitable for use in the freezer, being either of thin plastic which may crack, or having ill-fitting lids which spring off unless sealed with tape. Liquid or semi-solid food frozen in plastic boxes must have HEADSPACE. See also SEALING.

Plums

Choose plums which are just ripe, wipe skins. Cut each plum in half and discard the stone. Pack in 30% or 40% SYRUP in a waxed carton, rigid polythene container or a polythene bag lining a sugar carton. Keep the fruit submerged by placing crushed greaseproof paper or cellophane on the top of the syrup. Leave HEADSPACE and seal, label.

Freezer Life. Up to 1 year.

To Use. Allow fruit to thaw in its freezer container overnight and use as required. Fruit may be cooked directly from the freezer.

Polythene bags

The most widely-used of all wrappings for frozen food. Extra-thick, heave-gauge bags with gussets are obtainable from specialized dealers. Perforated rolls of thinner polythene bags are obtainable in two convenient sizes, and are suitable for short-term storage. It is advisable to keep a stock of bags in small, medium and large sizes, rather than a collection of one size. Bags which have not been torn or holed can be washed, dried and re-used. Liquid or semi-solid food frozen in bags should be placed in rectangular cardboard sugar containers, etc., until frozen. Leave HEADSPACE.

Pork

Pork has a shorter FREEZER LIFE (about 3 months) than other butcher's meat, owing to its fatty composition. The idea that pork is an 'unhealthy' meat to eat in the summer is a throw-back to pre-refrigeration days, when it was the first meat to go bad in hot weather. Whatever the temperature of conditions of storage, pork will become RANCID, after a limited period of time. The fat becomes ill-flavoured itself, but rancidity does not make food 'bad' in the food poisoning sense. Cooked pork, or dishes with pork included, should not be stored in a home freezer for more than 2 months. See also MEAT, PURCHASE OF,—FREEZING,—PACKING, CASSEROLES, BACON, HAM.

Positioning of a home freezer

A freezer need not necessarily be kept in the kitchen. It can be positioned in any dry place—garage, laundry-room, out-house, covered porch, understair space—and requires only 2 clear inches of space next to the condenser to allow circulation of air. Ideally, a freezer should be positioned away from sources of heat, on grounds of economy of running. Continuous damp may affect the casing and eventually the mechanical and electrical components.

Potted shrimps

Freshly-boiled shrimps can be potted in butter, according to any favoured recipe, and kept in the freezer. Most recipes call for mace to be used, and rather more than the suggested amount may well be included—likewise pepper, though not much extra salt should be included. If ready-frozen peeled shrimps are used, they should not be allowed to thaw before being put into the butter, but the block broken up and used as nearly frozen as possible.

Freezing. Glass jars must not be used, in case of shattering. Small aluminium foil or plastic dishes will hold a double serving of potted shrimps, the dishes filled to within a quarter-inch of the top and covered with a piece of foil.

Replace the lid and seal with a cross of sticky tape. Label. *Freezer Life*. Up to 5 months.

To Use. Take the pots from the freezer about 3 hours before serving, remove lid and foil, cover dishes with a cloth and leave at room temperature until required. Do not refreeze shrimps as the flavour will be very poor after thawing.

Poultry

See individual entries for CHICKEN and TURKEY, also GAME, DUCK, GOOSE.

Poultry—leftovers

As MEAT LEFTOVERS.

Power cuts

In case of electricity failure at the mains, *do not open the freezer*. A fully-loaded, unopened freezer will maintain a sufficiently low temperature for many hours—maybe up to a day in the case of a large model which is full of food. Check the cause of the failure, e.g. switch, fuse, before telephoning for help. If a power cut looks like lasting for more than four or five hours, cover the whole freezer with blankets to give as much insulation as possible. It is known for freezer owners to have an emergency arrangement with an obliging shopkeeper, whereby the contents of a failed or cut-off freezer can be rushed to temporary refuge in a sales cabinet or conservator.

Pre-cooked food

Food cooked for the freezer *must* be thoroughly cooled before being put into its freezer container by standing a metal or ovenproof cooking pot in cold water—it should not be left lingering before freezing. Warm food will transmit heat to frozen food already in the freezer, possibly with undesirable results. Pre-cooked food—particularly a party dish which needs to be kept tidy and all of a piece—can conveniently be frozen in its serving dish if the dish is lined with KITCHEN FOIL before freezing. When the food is solidly frozen, the foil package is lifted out and stored with an overwrapping of polythene. Put the package back in the dish for reheating, and slide the foil out before serving.

Pulses

Preparation. Choose dried beans, peas and lentils from a shop with a quick turnover of the goods, or you may be buying dusty relics of the past. Soak and cook pulses in the ordinary way, but only to the point where they are *just* tender and would not be quite ready for immediate eating. Drain and cool by standing in a colander under the running cold tap. Dry by shaking and patting gently with a tea-cloth or absorbent kitchen paper.

Freezing. Pulses should be frozen in plastic boxes or rigid containers such as waxed milk cartons or margarine containers, leaving a little HEADSPACE. If they are squashed by heavier items during storage, their appearance is not appetizing.

Freezer Life. Up to 6 months.

To Use. Butter and haricot beans, for serving as an extra vegetable, are heated in a double boiler or in a bowl over a pan of simmering water, with a large lump of butter set to melt on top. Peas and lentils, for use as soup additions, are put directly into the soup pan, where their cooking is completed. These can also be puréed after thawing and blended with STOCK to make thick soup.

Quantities for freezing

It is difficult, and sometimes impossible, to divide large quantities of pre-cooked and frozen food without breaking and spoiling the ingredients and the look of the food. Prepared food should be measured out into what counts as a normal-size serving dish for the household, and that quantity frozen in each container.

Rabbit

Preparation. If the rabbits have not been prepared by the butcher, eviscerate them as soon as possible after killing, and hang them head-downwards in a cool place for several hours. Skin and draw, wash thoroughly inside and out with lightly salted cold water and wipe dry. Rabbits can be frozen whole and uncooked, but jointing before freezing reduces the thawing time. When cooking rabbits for the freezer, do not include any bacon or pork, fresh or pickled, at first cooking if the rabbits are to be kept for more than 6–8 weeks. Being dry, jointed rabbits are best cooked slowly in the oven in a well-flavoured STOCK, with a BOUQUET GARNI or chopped fresh or frozen HERBS to taste. Season with salt and freshly ground black pepper, add a bay leaf and some fine strips of lemon rind to the dish. When the meat is just tender, cool the dish by putting the lidded pan under running cold water, or turning the food out of an oven dish into a bowl and standing it in another bowl of cold water with ice cubes.

Freezing. Wrap whole, uncooked rabbits, or joints, in foil, wadding any sharp bones with polythene or greaseproof paper, and overwrap in a polythene bag. Expel all air by pressing the polythene against the foil package, seal and label. Cooked rabbit should be immersed in its own cooking stock in a plastic bowl or box, leaving HEADSPACE, sealed and labelled.

Freezer Life. 6–8 months.

To Use. Thaw uncooked rabbit in the refrigerator overnight, leaving it covered at room temperature for an hour or two before cooking. Put frozen cooked rabbit into an ovenproof dish or casserole, reheat in a slow oven until thawed, then cover with a mixture of fresh or frozen breadcrumbs, parsley, thyme, a little sage, all mixed with melted butter. Spoon some of the cooking liquor over the top. Raise the heat just enough to crisp the topping without overcooking the meat or drying the juices.

Ragout

See CASSEROLES. The preliminary browning of the meat should be done in oil or luxury margarine, rather than butter, if the dish is prepared in quantity for freezing.

Preparation. For 4 portions trim and cut 1½ lb. chuck steak into large cubes. Cut 4 onions and 4 carrots into quarters. Crush 1 clove garlic in a little salt. Heat 2 tablespoons of oil in a thick casserole and fry meat quickly to brown all sides. Remove the meat and add onions. Fry more slowly until just beginning to brown. Sprinkle 1 oz. flour over the onion, add 1 pint beef STOCK, the crushed garlic and 1 tablespoon TOMATO PURÉE. Stir, bring to the boil, replace meat and add BOUQUET GARNI. Cover and simmer gently for about 1½ hours, adding the carrot after the first ¾ hour. Remove the bouquet garni.

Freezing. Stand the tightly-lidded casserole under running cold water and cool completely. Place the ragout in a foil-lined dish or in rigid plastic containers. Cover and freeze. Remove foil package and overwrap in a polythene bag. Seal and label.

Freezer Life. 4–6 months.

To Use. Remove foil package from polythene bag and allow ragout to stand at room temperature for about ½–1 hour. Peel off foil and place food in a thick saucepan. Heat gently until thoroughly hot. Just before serving add 2 tablespoons sherry.

Ragu

Preparation. Make ragu in multiples of the basic quantity: 12 oz. of minced beef, 6 oz. of chicken livers, a carrot, an onion, 1 large or 2 small sticks of celery, 3 tablespoons each of TOMATO PURÉE, white wine and STOCK. Cubes of bacon or uncooked ham are added if liked, before or after freezing. Chop the vegetables finely and brown them in three or four tablespoons of olive oil in a thick stewpan. Add the minced meat, turning it about in the oil until it browns. Put in the quartered chicken livers and tomato purée. Moisten well with

WINE (which see) and STOCK. Cover the pan and simmer the mixture very gently until the sauce is thick and rich, but not too reduced. Season with salt, freshly ground black pepper and chopped marjoram. Turn out of the pan into a bowl and cool thoroughly.

Freezing. Put the sauce in serving quantities into plastic or waxed containers, leaving HEADSPACE. Seal and label. This quantity will fit into two 1-pint wax cartons.

Freezer Life. Up to 2 months with bacon. 3 or 4 months without bacon.

To Use. Turn the sauce out of freezer containers into a saucepan, stirring frequently to avoid scorching when it begins to thaw, or re-heat in a covered bowl over a pan of simmering water. Add cubes of cooked bacon or ham if not already included, adjust seasoning. Use with pasta.

Rancid, Rancidity

Food which is termed 'rancid' is not 'bad' in the sense of being decomposed, rotten or poisonous if consumed. Rancid food is, however, unpleasant in taste, smell and occasionally in appearance. The high salt content of cured meat—bacon or ham—hastens similar changes. Home-frozen food cooked with a large quantity of butter is also subject to rancidity after over-long storage.

Rancidity occurs in foods containing fat—the more fat that is present, the more quickly will undesirable changes be detected. Rancidity is most often caused by oxidation and by enzyme activity.

Raspberries

Preparation. Raspberries selected for freezing must be quite dry and as direct from the cane as can possibly be managed. Town shop-bought raspberries, which must be presumed to have been in transit and often handled for at least 24 hours, are likely to prove a sad disappointment. Pick the fruit over most carefully, discarding any berries with the slightest trace of mould, or any squashed ones from the bottom of the basket, or any which have been bitten by worms. Do not on any account wash the fruit—if it is dirty enough to be washed, it is too dirty to be frozen.

Freezing. Put 1 or 1¼ lb. quantities of fruit loosely into polythene bags, tie and place the bags flat on a wire baking tray inside the freezer for an hour or two. When the fruit is firm, ease all the berries down the bag without lumping them too much together, press as much air as possible out of the bag with the finger-tips, and tie the neck of the bag firmly with a plastic-covered wire tie. Stack the frozen bags tidily for storage. Alternatively pack in rigid polythene containers.

To Use. If the fruit is to be eaten at lunch-time, take the required quantity out of the freezer and leave in its bag in the refrigerator overnight, turning the fruit out on to a dish in the middle of the morning. For tea or dinner, take the fruit out of the freezer 4 or 5 hours ahead of time and leave on a covered dish at room temperature. Do not hasten thawing by heating the fruit. Perfectly thawed raspberries still have a trace of the ice about them. Hustled or over-thawed fruit will collapse.

Ratatouille

Preparation. Ratatouille is a fragrant vegetable mixture, Provençal in origin, which can be served hot with cold meat or meat pies, or as an alternative to a plain vegetable with roast meat, steaks or chops, or cold as an hors d'oeuvre. Prepare for the freezer in multiples of the basic quantities—2 aubergines, 2 courgettes, 1 lb. of tomatoes, 1 or 2 green peppers, 1 onion, 4 cloves of garlic, 3 or 4 tablespoons of olive oil, chopped basil, marjoram and a little thyme to taste. Slice the aubergines and courgettes, skin the tomatoes and cut in slices. Take out seeds and membrane from the peppers and slice thinly. Slice the onion thinly, heat the oil in a large thick stewpan and drop in the crushed garlic, taking care that it does not become brown. Add the onion and cook until beginning to soften. Add the courgettes and aubergines, turning them over gently in the oil. After 10 minutes, put in the sliced peppers, and 10 minutes later still the tomatoes. Season well with herbs, salt and freshly ground black pepper. Cover the pan, reduce the heat and simmer the mixture until all the vegetables are tender but not mushy, and the liquid well reduced and full of flavour. Turn into a bowl and stand it in a bowl of cold water until the ratatouille is quite cold.

Freezing. Put the ratatouille into waxed or plastic containers, or into polythene bags, leave HEADSPACE, seal and label.

Freezer Life. Up to 6 months.

To Use. Turn the ratatouille out of the containers into a thick saucepan and reheat gently. Take care not to let the vegetables become dry or scorched. Taste for seasoning before serving. If the dish is to be served cold, leave the closed container at room temperature overnight.

Ravioli

Preparation. Buy freshly-made, small ravioli from a delicatessen or Italian provision merchant. Store in the freezer—do not cook before freezing.

Freezer Life. 4–6 months.

To Use. When required, put the ravioli straight from the freezer into a pan of simmering STOCK and cook until the pasta swells and rises in the cooking liquor, most of which will be absorbed. While the pasta is cooking, thaw an appropriate quantity of TOMATO PURÉE, add to the cooked ravioli with its remaining liquid. Cook gently, avoiding scorching or drying, until all is very hot. Serve with grated Parmesan cheese. Check seasoning of the sauce before serving.

Redcurrants

Preparation. Do not attempt to freeze redcurrants which were picked in damp weather, or those which look wet and pink instead of the desirable translucent red. String the currants, discarding any with traces of mould or broken skins. If they *must* be washed, the washing should be done after stringing, to avoid too much handling when the fruit is wet and vulnerable. Put the fruit in a colander or wire basket gently to avoid squashing the fruit. Since redcurrants are usually served as a cooked pudding, freezing them uncooked preserves freedom of choice of method later on.

Freezing. Put the currants in 1 or 1½ lb. quantities in polythene bags, and lay the bags flat on wire cake cooling trays inside the freezer until the fruit is completely frozen. Shake the frozen fruit down in the bags, without making a bulky package, press out as much air as possible by smoothing the bags upwards from the bottom. Tie the necks of the bags firmly with plastic-coated wire ties.

Freezer Life. Up to 1 year.

To Use. Leave the redcurrants in the bag in the refrigerator overnight, turning out on to a dish and leaving at room temperature for 2–3 hours to complete the thawing. If the fruit is to be stewed or made into a pie or steamed pudding, it can be used directly from the freezer. If the bags are frozen and stored flat, the fruit will not stick together and will run easily out of the bag. Perfect specimens of redcurrants can be frosted with egg white and sugar and used as decoration for a dish. Frost the berries just before thawing is complete, and use immediately.

Refreezing

Raw food taken from the freezer can be cooked and refrozen. Its eating quality (texture and flavour) will not be improved, but will probably be acceptable. If frozen prepared food is thawed and heated in excess of immediate needs, the surplus can be cooled and refrozen providing there is no delay and the food is *not* kept warm or standing at room temperature. From the eating point of view, refreezing cannot be recommended

145

and is unsuitable for fish, minced meat products and vegetables.

Reheating frozen food

Be sure to heat foods thoroughly but not for longer than necessary as the flavour will be spoiled. Take care that sauces do not dry. See also OVERCOOKING.

Rhubarb

Garden-grown rhubarb with a very good flavour may be frozen after gentle cooking in a 30% or 40% sugar SYRUP. Cool thoroughly before packing in rigid polythene containers with HEADSPACE. Seal and label.

Freezer Life. Up to 1 year.

To Use. If rhubarb is to be served as a dessert with cream or custard allow to thaw in unopened container for 2–3 hours. Rhubarb can also be used as the basis for a crumble in which case it should be thawed just enough to allow it to be spread in the cooking dish. Proceed as for APPLE CRUMBLE.

Rice

Preparation. Put 1 lb. of rice in at least 8 pints of water; add 2 tablespoonfuls of salt. Bring to the boil, reduce heat slightly and cook for 11 minutes. Drain off water, replace rice in pan and cover with tea-towel and pan lid. Leave in a warm place for 15 minutes stirring once or twice.

Freezing. Pack loosely in a polythene bag, and seal with a wire-covered tie. Place in the freezer. When grains are half-frozen, squeeze the bag gently to separate the mass. When solid, seal and tie with HEADSPACE.

Freezer Life. 4–6 months.

To Use. Frozen rice can be dropped into hot soup, which is then brought back to the boil. For serving as an accompaniment, allow rice to stand at room temperature $\frac{1}{2}$–1 hour. Spread on an ovenproof dish, and add a few knobs of butter. Heat, covered with foil, in the oven at 275°–300° F. (Gas Mark 2) until hot throughout.

Rissoles

See MEAT—LEFTOVERS.

Root vegetables

Potatoes, onions, turnips, and swedes are available either all the year round, or in ample season, and may not be considered worth freezing. The only exceptions among root vegetables are baby beetroots and carrots. See individual entries.

Runner beans

Preparation. It is unwise to freeze runner beans bought from a town shop, which will be inferior to the ready-frozen variety

146

bought in bulk from a frozen-food supplier. Home-grown beans should be picked and frozen while very young, long before they have become bent and tough. String the beans, cut and BLANCH for 2 minutes.

Freezing. Put the blanched beans into polythene bags, tie loosely. Freeze the bags flat on a wire tray in the freezer until they are firm, then separate the contents by gently shaking the bag or pressing it with the fingertips. Seal firmly with a plastic-covered wire tie. Before freezing, do not press the beans down into a lump, which will be inconvenient for later cooking.

Freezer Life. Up to 1 year.

To Use. Cook the beans directly from the freezer, in a small quantity of fast-boiling salted water for no more than 7–10 minutes.

Running costs

The running costs of a freezer vary slightly in different districts, according to local charges for electricity. As a general guide, each cubic foot of freezer will use about 3–5 units of electricity per week. Running costs are kept to a minimum if the freezer is not opened more often than is necessary, and the lid or door never left open for more than a few moments at a time. An eight cubic foot freezer may cost about 25p (5s.) a week to run.

Safeguards

See WARNING DEVICES, also SWITCHES.

Salmon

Prepare, pack and freeze as FISH. A whole salmon can be bought at a favourable price in early summer, divided into cutlets or baking-size pieces. If it is to be served cold with a salad, or *en gelée*, it should be prepared before freezing, the skin removed and the fish carefully packed in a foil-lined ovenproof dish for freezing. Take out the foil pack when the fish is solidly frozen, and overwrap in polythene or pack in a plastic box. Prepare a mayonnaise separately before serving. A frozen salmon dish should be thawed in the refrigerator overnight, and left covered at room temperature for an hour or two before serving.

Freezer Life. Up to 8 weeks if frozen immediately after being caught—less if salmon was bought from a fish-monger.

Salt

Although the free-running table salt in common usage is satis-factory for use in foods to be frozen many people consider that unrefined natural sea-salt affords a better flavour. Rock

147

salt can be bought from high-class grocers, or from health food shops. The kind of salt described as being for bathing purposes is as good as that sold in smaller packets for cooking purposes, and rather cheaper. Rock salt need not be put through a grinder for use in cooking, but should be ground for table use. See also SEASONING.

Sandwiches

Sandwiches made for freezing and later use should have their crusts cut off and the sandwiches packed in layers in plastic boxes or polythene bags, the layers separated by greaseproof paper. Any conventional filling will freeze, with the exception of lettuce, cucumber, hard-boiled egg and mayonnaise, and tomato.

Freezer Life. Up to 6 weeks.

To Use. Sandwiches with thin bread will take about 1 hour at room temperature to thaw, thicker ones will need longer.

Sauces

Most sauces freeze well, the exceptions are those based on an emulsion such as hollandaise, which require commercially-prepared stabilizers to stop them from separating on freezing. MEAT SAUCE, ONION SAUCE, CHEESE SAUCE, plain WHITE SAUCES will freeze and thaw and in good condition. See individual entries. Do not overseason before freezing but adjust this during reheating. Do not freeze corn-flour-thickened sauces as these will become very gelatinous and unappetizing.

Sausage rolls

Preparation. Ready-prepared frozen sausage rolls can be purchased in bulk, or they can be made with bought frozen or home-made and frozen pastry. Press the edges firmly together with the fingers, rather than use water or milk. Do not brush with egg or milk before freezing uncooked. Cool cooked rolls.

Freezing. Pack a large quantity of sausage rolls in a plastic box, placing them in layers with foil between. Leave sufficient room at the top of the box so that any pressure on the lid will not squash the rolls.

Freezer Life. 2–3 months—the life of the sausages, not the pastry.

To Use. Set the rolls on a baking tray, brush with milk or egg beaten with salt, cook direct from the freezer in a hot oven. Unless the rolls are very small, allow a little extra cooking time to ensure that the sausages are thoroughly cooked. Cooked rolls can be thawed for about 2 hours at room temperature, or $\frac{1}{2}$ hour in the warming drawer of the cooker.

Sausages

Sausages from the butcher can be frozen as soon as they are brought home, but in quantities no larger than 1 lb. per package, or they will freeze into an unmanageable mass. A pound-string should be put lengthways into a polythene bag folded back upon itself to divide the quantity and speed the thawing process. Sausages from the freezer can be put directly into a moderate oven to cook, without thawing first. Sausages for frying should be thawed in the refrigerator, or their cooking time will be too long for convenience. Frankfurter sausages bought in large economy-size cans can be divided into smaller quantities and frozen. See also SAUSAGE ROLLS.

Freezer Life. Up to 3 months.

Sealing

It is important that all containers and bags used for freezing food should be firmly sealed—partly for the obvious reason of stopping the food from falling out, partly to retain the flavour of the packed food, partly to prevent the food from becoming dry and brittle through long exposure to very cold air. Polythene bags are sealed with plastic-covered wire ties. The wire is twisted round the neck of the bag about an inch from the top, the top then turned down and the wire twisted round the fold. The wire ties are available in tubes of 50 from main branches of large stationers or from stockists of freezer containers. They are also sometimes included in packs or rolls of polythene bags. The ties can almost always be used several times over. The tight closure on good quality lidded plastic containers, such as Tupperware, is usually an adequate seal in itself. Cheaper plastic containers, though most useful because inexpensive and available in a wide range of sizes, should have sticky tape fastened round the lid if the contents are liquid or highly-seasoned or particularly prone to drying, as cooked meat. Foil-wrapped parcels of food frozen in a casserole or stewpot should be sealed in several places with freezer tape or masking tape from a do-it-yourself decorating shop which is cheaper and often equally effective.

Seasoning

Only personal taste decides whether food for the freezer should be more or less highly seasoned than that for immediate consumption. In general terms, however, garlic should be slightly more liberally used in freezer dishes. Dried herbs do not always retain a true flavour during freezer storage, but fresh ones can be relied upon. In particular thyme and sage increase in flavour intensity during frozen storage. Rock salt tends to develop the flavour of meat, fish and poultry, or vegetable dishes, better than table salt. Freshly-ground black pepper, except where the dark grains might spoil the appearance of a pale sauce, should always be used in preference to ready-ground white pepper. All seasonings—curry powder, gravy browning, mustard, herbs and spices—should be as fresh as possible. They should be bought in small quantities from a shop with a brisk trade, to reduce the possibilities of their having had a long shelf-life already, and stored in airtight containers. For the new freezer owner, a good rule is to season foods no more highly than usual. In most cases seasoning can be increased during the reheating operation if necessary.

Second-hand or reconditioned freezers

It is not a good idea to buy a freezer on these terms. The motor may be old or defective, the guarantee long-ago run out, the casing doctored to conceal rusty or cracked places, the insurance rates too high to be an economic proposition. Shortcomings will not be apparent until the freezer is in operation, or proves inoperative, and the purchaser will have no redress.

Scones

Home-made or shop-bought scones, plain or fruit, can be frozen before or after cooking, in polythene bags. Interleave uncooked scones with foil or polythene.
Freezer Life. Up to 3 months.
To Use. Thaw cooked scones at room temperature for about 1 hour or in a warming drawer or low oven for about 15 minutes. Scones can be toasted direct from the freezer. If they are to be split and buttered, cut them through horizontally before freezing, to speed up thawing.

Scotch eggs

Having hard-boiled eggs at their heart, Scotch eggs are NON-FREEZERS.

Shellfish

Preparation. Only the very freshest of shellfish should be prepared for freezing—that bought from a seaside fishmonger, or even a fisherman, or bought already frozen solid and put straight into the freezer. Choose crabs and lobsters that feel heavy for their size, mussels with tightly-closed shells, scampi that looks and feels firm, not flaccid, shrimps and prawns likewise. *If in doubt, or a hundred miles from the sea, do not buy shellfish for freezing.* Cook shellfish in the usual way. Remove all meat from crabs and lobsters, keeping white and dark meat and coral apart. Wash mussels, simmer a few moments in wine or water until the shells open. Wash, boil and peel scampi, prawns and shrimps. Discard any which are broken or soft. Do not leave shellfish at room temperature or even in the refrigerator for any length of time before freezing.

Freezing. Freeze lobster and crab meat in plastic containers or waxed cartons, separating the different kinds of meat with layers of foil inside the container. These two kinds of shellfish can, at a pinch, be frozen entire in their shells after cooking, wrapped in foil and overwrapped in a polythene bag. Seal and label all bags and containers. Pack scampi, shrimps and prawns in polythene bags, tightly sealed at the neck and labelled with weight and date. After cooking take mussels out of their shells, cool in a bowl standing in cold water, pack with their juices in plastic or waxed containers with HEADSPACE, seal tightly and label.

Freezer Life. Not more than 2–3 months, but up to 5 months for prawns/shrimps.

To Use. Leave the packages unopened in the refrigerator for several hours, bringing out and standing covered at room temperature before serving. Lobster meat should be completely thawed before putting into sauce for serving as Thermidor, Américaine or Newburg.

Shepherd's pie

Preparation. Each 1 lb. meat will require 1 teaspoon dry mustard, 1 large onion, salt, pepper, 4 tablespoons TOMATO PURÉE, 4 oz. bacon, 1 lb. mashed potato.

Mince leftover meat immediately after first cooking. Mix with the mustard. Chop the onion and bacon and fry gently. Boil potatoes and mash with a little milk and butter. Cool. Add cooked bacon, onion, tomato purée and seasoning to meat. If the mixture seems at all dry, add a little beef stock.

Freezing. Place meat in a deep foil baking dish. Cover with mashed potato, freeze. Overwrap in a polythene bag. Seal and label.

Freezer Life. Up to 2 months, or 6 weeks if bacon is added before freezing.

To Use. Remove polythene bag and heat shepherd's pie in the oven at 425°F. (Gas Mark 7) for about 1 hour until hot throughout. It may be necessary to brown the potato under the grill.

Situation of a home freezer

See POSITIONING OF A HOME FREEZER.

Snipe	See GAME.
Sole	*Preparation*. See FISH. Sole quickly loses its best flavour after being caught, so only the very freshest should be frozen. Skinning or scaling, and gutting, should be done before freezing. Sole can be frozen in fillets or on the bone, but does not repay cooking before freezing.

Sole (continued)

Freezing. Interleave 3–4 fillets, or 1–2 fish, wrap closely in foil to make a neat parcel. Make other matching parcels and freeze several overwrapped in a polythene bag. Seal and label.

Freezer Life. 3–4 months.

To Use. Cook the sole as soon as the pieces have thawed sufficiently to be separated without damage.

Solid packs

Referring to some commercially-frozen vegetables, bought in bulk, which are frozen in a solid brick. When available, FREE-RUNNING PACKS, which see, should be ordered for a home freezer, otherwise cooking quantities will have to be broken from the mass, with consequent wastage and crushing of the vegetables.

Soufflés

Preparation. Cold, sweet soufflés or MOUSSES, can be prepared to any favoured recipe and frozen. Hot soufflés would sink during the required cooling before freezing, and thus are not to be considered as home-freezer material. Double cream can be used where called for by a recipe, but 'whipping cream' will give a longer-lasting result in freezer terms. If the mixture will stand it, rather more sugar than usual should be mixed in a soufflé which is to be frozen. Chill in the refrigerator until set.

Freezing. Soufflés must never be frozen in glass or china dishes, which would probably break inside the freezer. Ovenproof china, oven-glass dishes or waxed paper cases must be used. If the soufflé has a paper band round a high-standing top, leave this in place during storage, with the additional protection of a wide doubled fence of foil to the same height and secured round the dish. Do not decorate the soufflé before freezing. If the freezer has a basket, stand the soufflé in a large polythene bag, closely sealed, on the bottom of the basket. Otherwise it should be placed in a deep polythene box, or a biscuit tin, with two crossed strips of doubled foil under the dish to act as handles for lifting. At all costs, avoid knocking a soufflé when reaching into the freezer for other items.

Freezer Life. As short as possible, owing to great pressure on space and possibility of damage.

To Use. Leave the soufflé still enclosed in its polythene bag, at room temperature for 2–3 hours before serving, according to size. Decorate with chopped nuts, whipped cream rosettes, etc., immediately before serving.

Soup

Preparation. Any meat or vegetable soup can be prepared in larger-than-usual quantity and the surplus frozen. Pieces of ham or bacon should not be left in soup such as minestrone, if it is to be kept for more than 6 weeks, and cream soup is better if any liaison of egg yolks and cream is stirred in at re-heating—it may otherwise separate in the freezer, or curdle in the pan. Cool and skim all excess fat before freezing.

Freezing. Soup can be frozen in plastic or waxed containers, leaving HEADSPACE, which see. It can be frozen in poly-thene bags, also with headspace, but they should either be laid flat during freezing or placed in 1 lb. sugar cartons to make a 'brick' shape.

Freezer Life. 2–3 months for meat soup, up to 6 months for vegetable.

To Use. Hold a rigid container under running hot water for a moment, when the contents will loosen and fall out. Stand a sealed polythene bag of soup in a bowl of cold water until the polythene loosens. Using a low heat at first, reheat meat or thick vegetable soup to boiling point in a saucepan, cream soup in a double-boiler or a bowl over a pan of simmering water, adding liaison immediately before serving.

Soup—puréed

Preparation. Puréed or cream soups are usually prepared from vegetables—lettuce, watercress, asparagus, spinach or leek, mushroom or tomato. Make in large quantities according to any favoured recipe, but if the vegetables are cooked in milk, reconstituted dried skim milk should be considered rather than whole milk. Follow the recipe to the point where milk, egg yolk, or cream would be added to the puréed vegetables, then cease the cooking. Cool the mixture before freezing, by standing the pan in a bowl of cold water.

Freezing. Pour the puréed vegetables into plastic or waxed containers, leaving HEADSPACE. Seal and label clearly as to contents.

Freezer Life. Up to 6 months.

To Use. Turn the mixture into a double saucepan or thick pan, thaw over gentle heat until the point is reached where cream, egg or milk can be stirred in. Do not allow the

153

thawed mixture to reach boiling point before the additions are made, or to boil afterwards. Adjust seasoning before serving.

Spaghetti

It is a waste of time to cook and freeze spaghetti as it takes hours to thaw and no more than 15 minutes to cook from scratch.

Similarly, it is a waste of time to make up spaghetti bolognese. It is far quicker to thaw and heat the appropriate sauce (MEAT, TOMATO, etc.) and pour this over freshly-cooked spaghetti.

Spinach

One of the vegetables much better bought in bulk ready-frozen than prepared at home for the freezer. If home-grown, a freezer quantity of spinach requires an enormous amount of garden space which could be put to more interesting use. Blanching and packing of spinach for home freezing is more time-consuming than the preparation of any other vegetable.

Spirits or liqueurs in freezer cooking

See WINE.

Star marking system

A method evolved by quick-frozen food producers and the British Standards Institution to indicate a recommended storage period for commercially quick-frozen foods in frozen food storage compartments of household refrigerators. Generally one star on the compartment indicates a recommended storage period of up to one week, two stars up to one month, and three stars up to three months. The above stated storage periods do not apply equally to all frozen foods, however, and packets of commercially frozen foods are marked with the actual recommended storage period for the particular product. Star marking does not apply to home freezers, which are designed to store home-frozen food for even longer periods of time.

Steaks

All cuts of steak for frying or grilling should be frozen flat, each piece separated from the next by a double piece of foil, cellulose film or greaseproof paper, and no more than two or three 1-inch-thick steaks packaged together. Place the packages in the coldest part of the freezer so that they are frozen rapidly, after which the packages can be conveniently stacked. Thaw overnight in the refrigerator if possible, leaving the meat in its freezer wrapping. If the meat *has* to be cooked direct from the freezer, start the cooking by gentle heat to thaw

154

the cut right through. Increase the heat when the meat feels tender to the touch.

Steamed puddings

Preparation. For freezer purposes, make a very large quantity of sponge pudding mixture, then divide the quantity into a given number of foil or polypropylene pudding basins. Flavour the divided mixture with cut-up glacé cherries or dried fruit, almond essence, chopped nuts or cooled melted chocolate marbled through the mixture. Fill the bowls to within one inch of the top.

Freezing. Cover the bowls with doubled squares of kitchen foil, pressing it under the convenient edges of the foil bowls or clip on the lids of plastic basins. Overwrap foil basins with polythene and label according to flavour.

Freezer Life. 3–4 months.

To Use. Steam the puddings directly from the freezer, allowing 2 hours cooking time for a 1 or 2 lb. pudding rather than the usual 1½ hours.

Stews

See CASSEROLES.

Stick beans

A regional name for RUNNER BEANS.

Stock

Preparation. Make jellied stock by boiling or pressure cooking marrow or veal bones with a couple of pig's trotters, some chicken necks, a large BOUQUET GARNI, quartered onions, carrots and celery sticks until the original quantity of water has been reduced by one-third. Strain the stock and leave it in a bowl in the refrigerator overnight. Take off the layer of fat from the top.

Freezing. Jellied stock can be frozen in polythene bags laid flat on wire trays inside the freezer until solidly frozen in a thin layer or in small waxed cartons, plastic containers or ice cube containers, leaving HEADSPACE.

Freezer Life. Up to 6 months.

To Use. Hold plastic or waxed containers under running hot water until the contents can be pushed out as the surface thaws. Stand polythene bags in a bowl of cold water until the polythene loosens.

Strawberries

Preparation. Choose firm, dry, unmarked strawberries for freezing. Vast, deep-red berries freeze less well than small ones, having a proportionately higher water content. Hull the berries, checking them at the same time for traces of insects. Discard berries with more than a speck or two of earth on them, which can be flicked off. Washing earth-stained berries will only result in their tasting of diluted mud, instead of the pure substance. It is not necessary or desirable to freeze strawberries in sugar or syrup, unless the thawed fruit is to be used in flans, when the excess of juices can be reduced by boiling to jelly.

Freezing. Put 1 or 1½ lb. quantities of fruit carefully into polythene bags, avoiding too much discrepancy in the size of fruit in each bag. Tie the bags loosely and place them flat on wire baking trays inside the freezer for an hour or two. When the fruit is firm, shake it down in the bags, press out as much air as possible, and tie the necks of the bags firmly with plastic-coated wire ties. Stack the bags neatly for storage or place them in rigid polythene boxes to protect berries from damage during storage.

Freezer Life. Up to 1 year.

To Use. Allow berries to thaw at room temperature in their container for up to three hours, serve slightly chilled or sprinkle with sugar before thawing to allow a syrup to form. Serve chilled.

Fruit may also be thawed for about 5 hours in the refrigerator.

Stuffing

Preparation. Parsley and thyme, sage and onion or chestnut stuffing can be prepared in the usual way for freezing. Forcemeat stuffing can also be prepared for freezing. If a large quantity of stuffing is made for freezing, the mixture should not be moistened unless serving quantities can be gauged. A mixture containing eggs and/or lemon juice will freeze solid and may be inconvenient if a fresh or already thawed bird is to be stuffed. Mix freshly prepared or already frozen breadcrumbs, parsley, herbs and seasoning.

Freezing. Pack a dry stuffing mixture in a large polythene bag, without HEADSPACE, seal and label according to ingredients, e.g., 'Sage', 'Parsley and Thyme'. *Stuffing must not be frozen inside a frozen fowl or joint of meat*, but may be frozen in small fish such as herrings, or in cutlets of fish.

Freezer Life. Dry mixtures, up to 6 months. If moistened and frozen in fish, according to the freezer life of the fish.

To Use. Measure out quantities of dry mixtures and use direct from the freezer. Mix with egg, lemon juice, suet, etc. and complete preparation in the usual way. Cook stuffed fish straight from the freezer, but ensure that the stuffing is cooked through.

Suet pudding	*Preparation*. Make suet puddings in double the usual quantity, to any favoured recipe. For freezer purposes, the flavour of savoury suet puddings is improved by adding rather more salt and pepper than usual, and a very little chopped fresh sage or thyme leaves. Cook the puddings in 1 lb. foil pudding basins, one in a pan of boiling water and another in a steamer pan over the top. Cool. Sweet suet pudding can also be prepared and frozen after an hour or two steaming. *Freezing*. Cover the cooked puddings with fresh pieces of foil. Leave them in their bowls, overwrapped in a polythene bag, sealed and labelled. *Freezer Life*. Up to 2 months. *To Use*. Put the puddings straight from the freezer into a steamer pan over boiling water, and steam until thoroughly hot—about 2 hours for a 1-pint pudding.
Sugar	Puddings, pies or fruit cooked for the freezer may require more sugar than if they were prepared for immediate consumption. This is largely a matter of taste, and is decided by a short period of trial and error. It is useful to keep one or two vanilla pods in a jar of sugar when cakes or puddings are often made for the freezer—the flavour of bottled vanilla essence seems to be inferior to that of the pod in frozen food.
Sweetbreads	As KIDNEYS, which see.
Switches	The electric point on which a home freezer depends should be guarded against accidental switching off, a more likely source of calamity than power failure or breakdown of the freezer mechanism. The electric switch should be covered with a large cross of thick sticking plaster, the words DON'T TOUCH written upon it. See also WARNING DEVICES.
Syrup	It is often recommended that soft fruit should be frozen in syrup made from sugar and water, but it should be borne in mind when making a decision about 'syrup or not' that soft fruit so frozen will be very moist. MELON, CHERRIES, GOOSEBERRIES, PLUMS, RHUBARB and APRICOTS benefit from being frozen in syrup. A 'light syrup' is made from multiples of 8 oz. sugar and 1 pint water called a 30% syrup. 'Medium' or 40% syrup is 13 oz. sugar and 1 pint water. 'Heavy' or 50% syrup is 20 oz. sugar and 1 pint water. The proportions remain constant whatever quantity is prepared. The sugar is dissolved in the water, brought to the boil for 1 minute only. The syrup must

157

be quite cold before use. The strength of syrup you use will depend on personal preference but the 30% and 40% are most often employed. See individual fruit entries.

Terrine

Preparation. A terrine of meat or game can be prepared for the freezer according to any favoured recipe, but the inclusion of pork or bacon or ham will reduce the freezer life. The following recipe has been shown to freeze well: Streaky bacon to line the terrine mould, 1 lb. of minced veal, 6 oz. sausage meat, 10 oz. of lamb's liver–minced, 2 oz. of fresh or frozen white breadcrumbs, 3 cloves of garlic–crushed, 2 tablespoons of fresh or frozen mixed herbs—parsley, thyme, chives, marjoram—and an onion. Chop the onion finely, mix with the minced meat, sausage and liver, add breadcrumbs, herbs, garlic, salt and pepper, mix and stir all together very thoroughly. Line a terrine dish or ovenproof casserole with foil, pressing it very smoothly against the sides of the dish and leaving an ample margin all round the top.

Press the meat mixture evenly down into the dish, put half a green bay leaf on top, cover with overlapping foil and the lid of the dish or casserole. Stand the dish in a baking tin of water and cook in a slow to moderate oven for 1½–2 hours. The meat should feel quite firm when pressed with a finger.

Cool by standing the cooking dish in a bowl of cold water. Put a plate on top of the meat and weight it down. When the meat has cooled, put the weighted dish in the refrigerator to chill. When quite cold remove from dish and cut the terrine into slices. Interleave with pieces of foil, and wrap in more foil.

Freezing. Overwrap the terrine closely in a polythene bag, expel all air, seal and label.

Freezer Life. 3–4 weeks.

To Use. Take the whole terrine, or slices, out of the freezer and leave in the refrigerator overnight. Allow to stand covered at room temperature for 3–4 hours before serving.

Thermostat

An automatic device for maintaining a specified air temperature in the freezer. It is set to the lowest temperature for freezing fresh food, reduced to 'Normal' for storage, and works automatically, operating the freezer motor according to the temperature of the air inside the freezer.

Toad in the hole

Preparation. Make batter according to recipe for YORKSHIRE PUDDINGS. Pour over uncooked sausages in a deep foil baking dish.

158

Freezing. Stand the dishes on a wire cake tray fixed level and secured inside the freezer. When the contents are frozen, overwrap in a polythene bag and seal.

Freezer Life. Up to 3 months, the freezer life of the sausage rather than the batter.

To Use. Cook the toad in the hole direct from the freezer in a hot oven, 450°F. (Gas Mark 8) allowing about 15 minutes extra cooking time. Test before the end of cooking to ensure that the sausages are well cooked.

Tomatoes

Frozen tomatoes are suitable only for use in cooking, not as a raw salad vegetable.

Preparation. Choose tomatoes under-ripe rather than over for freezing. Discard any with bruises or soft sections. Skin by dropping the tomatoes into boiling water for a count of twelve, pouring off the water and replacing it with cold. The skins will come off in one piece in the fingers, and a knife need not be used. Cut the tomatoes into slices if large, into halves or quarters if of average size. Some very firm, very small specimens may be frozen whole. Cool before freezing.

Freezing. Pack the tomatoes into polythene bags, or rigid polythene boxes in quantities likely to serve for making soup or adding to casseroles where canned tomatoes would otherwise be used. Leave HEADSPACE, seal and label.

Freezer Life. Up to 1 year.

To Use. Use in cooked dishes directly from the freezer.

Tomato purée

Preparation. Cut ripe tomatoes in half horizontally and put them cut-side down in layers in a preserving pan, with chopped onions, basil or marjoram, half a green bay leaf, garlic, salt and ground black pepper, according to taste. Do not add water, but seethe and simmer the contents of the pan for an hour. Stir and crush from time to time. Press the cooked pulp through a nylon sieve rather than using a blender, which does not produce such a smooth texture in the purée. Return the purée to the pan and boil uncovered until the mixture is rich and thick. Cool and taste for seasoning.

Freezing. This purée is highly concentrated, and half the quantity should be frozen in small plastic cartons, such as cream cartons, covered with pieces of foil and with HEADSPACE. These small quantities are sufficient for flavouring soup, meat, poultry or vegetable dishes. Freeze the rest in larger quantities, in half-pound margarine containers, to pour over pasta or for use in RAGU.

Freezer Life. Up to 1 year.

To Use. Run the containers under the hot tap until the contents can be pushed out as the surfaces thaw.

Tomato sauce

Preparation. This is a sauce for pasta or meat dishes, being less smooth than a purée and quicker to prepare. Make for freezing in multiples of the basic recipe: 4 tablespoons olive oil, about 2 lb. of tomatoes skinned, cut in halves or quarters and most of the seeds squeezed out, 1 large onion, chopped finely, $\frac{1}{2}$ pint STOCK, 3 cloves of crushed garlic, 3 tablespoons TOMATO PURÉE, fresh or already frozen chopped basil or marjoram, a little flour, sugar, salt and ground black pepper. Soften the onion in the oil, sprinkle the flour into the pan and stir for 1 minute before blending in the stock and bringing briefly to the boil. Put in the tomatoes, herbs and seasonings. Cook gently until the sauce is well reduced and pulpy. Cool before freezing.

Freezing. Put the sauce in convenient quantities in waxed or plastic containers, or in polythene bags lining cardboard cartons, leave HEADSPACE. Seal and label.

Freezer Life. Up to 1 year.

To Use. Turn the sauce out of containers into a thick saucepan, break up lightly with a fork when beginning to thaw, stir to avoid scorching. Adjust seasoning before serving.

Trout

Freshly-caught trout can be cleaned and frozen whole in polythene bags. If more than one fish is to be frozen, separate each from the other by a piece of foil or greaseproof paper. Otherwise, once frozen, they will stick together and it will be necessary to force them apart and probably break the frozen flesh. Place the packages close to the walls of the freezer until they are solidly frozen, after which they can be conveniently stacked. See precautions and warnings under FISH.

Freezer Life. Up to 2 months.

Turbot

Preparation. See FISH. Cut turbot into steaks, wash in lightly salted water for freezing uncooked.

Freezing. Interleave steaks with polythene, foil or cellophane film and wrap in foil. Overwrap in a polythene bag, carefully expel all air by patting the bag round the cooked fish, seal and label.

Freezer Life. No more than 2 months.

To Use. Cook the fish direct from the freezer on a plate over a pan of simmering water, or poach and use cooking liquor to make sauce.

Turkeys	Pack and freeze as CHICKEN, which see. Turkeys can often be bought before the Christmas rush at less than peak price, but it is important to ascertain that the bird has not previously been frozen and thawed before sale. Also, bear in mind the size of the usual family bird—it will occupy a good deal of freezer space at a time when space is at a premium. A turkey weighing more than about 12 lb. should be allowed to thaw at room temperature for *at least* 72 hours before cooking. The bird should not be stuffed before freezing. During thawing time, the bird should be left in its polythene bag which should be opened, the whole should be covered with a clean towel. Turkey has a freezer life of 4–6 months.
Underwrapping	A term referring to the covering of greaseproof paper, polythene or even wadded tissue paper at a pinch, used to cover projecting bones, wings of poultry or meat, which might otherwise pierce their outer wrapping and allow air into the package. Also refers to the practice of wrapping food in foil before putting the foil package inside a polythene bag—as with CHOPS, STEAKS, POULTRY joints, or cooked food frozen in foil-lined dishes. Kitchen foil should be avoided for wrapping projecting bones, etc. Its edges may cut the outer polythene wrapping.
Upright freezers	An upright freezer looks like a refrigerator, externally. The contents are held either on fixed shelves or in pull-out baskets or a combination of both. The door may also serve as a food storage space. An upright freezer requires less floor space than the equivalent capacity CHEST-TYPE freezer. Some models have a fast-freeze compartment for the rapid freezing of foods.
Veal	The lean, firm flesh of veal freezes well in all its cuts. If a dish of veal is cooked for the freezer, it is important to prepare ample sauce or gravy, to offset the possible drying effect of freezing on an already dry meat. See also MEAT, PURCHASE OF, FREEZING, PACKING, BLANQUETTE OF VEAL, ESCALOPES OF VEAL. *Freezer Life*. Raw veal up to 9 months.
Vegetables	All vegetables intended for cooking before consumption *can* be frozen, but not all of them *should* be. Cabbage, potatoes, etc., which are available all the year round, are a waste of freezer space. Vegetables bought in a town shop or market are not likely to be worth freezing, because they will have

been harvested for much longer than the four hours which is the ideal maximum for freezing. This does not apply, however, to imported seasonal vegetables such as peppers, aubergines and artichokes. Nearly all vegetables must be subjected to BLANCHING. Also see individual entries.

Vegetables—leftovers Leftover vegetables should not be frozen or refrozen, because they will have a warmed-up taste.

Velouté sauce *Preparation*. A quantity of velouté sauce can be prepared for freezing in multiples of the basic quantity: 2 oz. butter, 2 oz. plain flour, ½ pint strained white STOCK, salt and pepper, a little lemon juice or vinegar. The liaison of 1 egg yolk and 4 tablespoons of double cream should, for the best results, be added during the final reheating. Cover the surface of the sauce with a piece of damped greaseproof paper and cool by standing the pan in a bowl of cold water.

Freezing. Place likely serving quantities in waxed or plastic containers, leaving HEADSPACE. Seal and label.

Freezer Life. Up to 6 months.

To Use. Turn the sauce out of container into a double boiler or a bowl over a pan of simmering water. Beat well during reheating but do not boil the sauce. Add egg yolk and cream if not already included.

Venison Venison is even more difficult to butcher than ordinary meat, and not a job to be attempted at home. Have it prepared for the freezer by the butcher, hung, and cut into joints. Pack and freeze as MEAT. The freezer life of venison is up to 8 months.

Vol-au-vent *Preparation*. Ready-frozen bouchées or *vol-au-vents* are nearly always preferable to the home-made variety—they are less expensive in terms of time and money, and do not collapse in cooking. But large pastry cases are as yet unobtainable from bulk suppliers of frozen foods. These can be made and frozen preferably raw, but cooked cases *can* be frozen. They are, however, very fragile and take up a great deal of freezer space. If frozen raw, the layers of pastry should not be brushed with milk or water to hold them together, and the cut-out centre section should be marked *before* freezing. Cool cooked cases before freezing.

Freezing. Raw pastry cases should be frozen flat on a cake tin or foil pie plate, lightly set into a plastic bag. Expel all air and seal when the pastry is quite firm. Cooked cases should be frozen in an amply-sized rigid plastic box, labelled 'With Care'.

Freezer Life. Raw puff pastry made with butter should not be stored for more than three months, as the butter may become rancid. Cooked pastry cases, if damage is avoided, will keep for many months if necessary.

To Use. Cook raw cases directly from the freezer in a hot oven. Leave cooked cases at room temperature for an hour or so before filling and serving.

Vol-au-vent fillings

Preparation. Frozen cooked chicken leftovers, or small quantities of leftover cooked game, or frozen chicken livers or prepared kidney in sauce or frozen mushrooms—all can be used as fillings for pastry cases.

Freezing. All the above items are taken to be frozen already.

To Use. Reheat the required quantity of WHITE SAUCE in a double-boiler or a bowl set over a pan of simmering water. Thaw required filling. Sauce and filling should be at about the same temperature before being mixed together. If the sauce has separated during reheating, it should be beaten smooth before the filling is added to avoid mashing the other ingredients. Taste for seasoning, possibly stir in some fresh cream, fill bouchées or *vol-au-vent* cases and heat throughout in a moderate oven.

Warning devices

Freezers which are out of sight or earshot, as in a garage, should be fitted with an alarm system which will operate as soon as the temperature within the freezer rises abnormally. A bell, buzzer and/or warning light can be operated from the mains electricity or from a battery. Fitting of such a device should be done only by a qualified electrician, and the cost will be upwards of £5. An absolutely vital precaution, without which a freezer load of food could be wasted.

Waxed containers

Wax-coated cardboard containers are manufactured for home-freezers in 1½ and 1 and 2 pint sizes, but they are expensive and cannot often be used more than once unless first lined with polythene bags. Waxed milk cartons can be bought by the gross from some dairies, and sealed for the freezer by two pieces of sticky tape being placed over the top fold of the carton. HEADSPACE, which see, should always be left between the surface of liquid or semi-liquid food and the top of a waxed container.

163

| Weight | A fully-loaded freezer weighs very heavily on the floor beneath it. Freezers of 12 cubic foot or over should stand on a foundation floor. The weight-bearing capacity of the floor should be checked by a builder if there is any doubt about its strength. In extreme cases it is possible to have floors strengthened by additional joists, as is done for grand pianos. |

White currants

Preparation. As REDCURRANTS.

White sauce

Preparation. For a savoury sauce, infuse 2 pints of milk, preferably reconstituted dried skim, with a dozen peppercorns, a little salt, a blade of mace, half a green bay leaf and a spoonful of finely chopped onion or shallot. Do not boil the milk, but leave it in the covered pan on a low heat for about 10 minutes. Make a roux of 3 oz. of margarine and 3 oz. of flour, cook until the mixture forms a ball and strain a third of the infused milk into the pan. Blend until smooth, add the rest of the milk and stir till boiling. Boil gently for a further 2–3 minutes. For a sweet sauce to serve with steamed pudding, infuse the milk with half a vanilla pod instead of seasoning and sweeten to taste before boiling. Cool the sauce by standing the pan in a bowl of cold water.

Freezing. Pour serving quantities of sauce into plastic or waxed containers, leaving HEADSPACE.

Freezer Life. Up to 6 months.

To Use. Hold the frozen containers under running hot water for a moment, push out the contents and reheat in a double boiler or a bowl over a pan of simmering water. The sauce may separate during freezing, but this has no effect on the taste and the consistency is restored by beating with a wooden spoon during reheating.

See individual entries for ONION, CHEESE, PARSLEY SAUCES, etc.

Wine

When a recipe calls for wine, reduce the quantity by about half if the dish is to be cooked for freezing. Freezer storage is known to affect the potency of wine as an ingredient, and some of the essential flavour will be lost. Make up the quantity when the dish is being reheated for serving. If spirits or liqueurs are called for, pour them over the reheated dish when the food is thoroughly hot to permeate the food exactly as if it had been an integral part of the cooking.

Wire trays

The oblong wire trays used for cooling cakes after cooking

can be used to hold soft fruit or delicate items inside the freezer during the freezing process. The food is thus supported and will freeze in good shape. The wire allows cold air to circulate on all sides of the packages, speeding the process and allowing the fruit to freeze individually.

Woodcock	See GAME.
Wrapping	All food for the freezer, raw or cooked, must be securely wrapped in moisture-vapour proof material—polythene bags or sheeting, kitchen foil or foil bowls and baking dishes, tightly lidded plastic bowls or boxes, waxed cardboard containers—and the package rendered as nearly air-tight as possible. Loosely wrapped packages allow the food to be damaged by rolling about, and the unprotected food dries out after constant contact with very cold air. Badly wrapped meat and fish may suffer 'freezer burn', resulting in greyish marks on the surface and spoiled flavour and texture. See also POLYTHENE, KITCHEN FOIL, PLASTIC BOXES, WAXED CONTAINERS. All packages should be wrapped to achieve as near to rectangular shape as possible, to save space in PACKING THE FREEZER.

Tubs originally containing margarine can be used for freezing food, being moisture-vapour proof, securely fastening and easily stacked. Liquid or semi-solid food can be poured into a polythene bag pressed down into a 1 or 2 lb. sugar or dried fruit carton, and frozen. The carton is then removed and the frozen brick of food stacked in the freezer. Make sure, by folding the top of the bag outside the edge of the carton, that no drops of food fall between the two surfaces. The drops will freeze and the bag will tear away with the carton. See also SEALING.

Yoghurt	Home-made or bought yoghurt will not freeze and thaw without separating. It should not be used in cooked dishes but you may be able to add it during reheating.
Yorkshire puddings	*Preparation.* Make Yorkshire puddings for the freezer in multiples of the basic quantity: 5 oz. of plain flour, $\frac{1}{2}$ teaspoon of salt, 1 egg, $\frac{1}{2}$ pint of liquid in the proportion of two-thirds milk and one-third water. Leave the prepared batter to stand at room temperature for about 1 hour, to allow the flour to swell in the liquid.

Freezing. Pour batter into lightly greased individual foil baking dishes, or deep tart cases, to come two-thirds of the

165

way up the dish. Fix a wire baking tray to stand level and secure inside the freezer, and put the uncovered dishes on it until the batter has frozen solid. Stack the frozen puddings in a polythene bag, seal.

Freezer Life. 3–4 months.

To Use. Cook the Yorkshire puddings direct from the freezer in a hot oven, allowing about 15 minutes extra cooking time.